LONDONOLOGY

A Deep Dive into the Worlds most Dynamic City

CHAPTER 1: THE GLOBAL CITY: AN INTRODUCTION TO MODERN LONDON

London. A name synonymous with royalty, red double-decker buses, and the iconic clock tower of Big Ben. Yet, this city is so much more than its tourist attractions. In the modern era, London has evolved into a dynamic global metropolis, pulsating with energy, diversity, and innovation.

London's global city status isn't merely a title—it's a living, breathing reality. The city's influence stretches far beyond its borders, shaping trends in finance, fashion, art, music, and technology. In the words of the renowned urbanist Saskia Sassen, London is a "command centre" of the global economy, a place where decisions made in gleaming skyscrapers reverberate through the world's stock markets.

Take a stroll through the Square Mile, London's historic financial district, and you'll see this global influence in action. The towering glass facades of international banks and financial institutions reflect the city's dominance in global finance. According to a 2023 report by the Global Financial Centres Index, London consistently ranks among the top three financial centres worldwide, alongside New York and Hong Kong.

But London's global influence isn't confined to the realm of finance. The city is also a cultural powerhouse, attracting talent and creativity from around the world. The West End, London's theatre district, rivals Broadway in terms of both prestige and ticket sales. Museums like the British Museum and the Tate Modern are home to world-class collections, drawing millions of visitors each year.

Fashion is another arena where London sets trends that ripple across the globe. From the avant-garde designs of Alexander McQueen to the high-street chic of Topshop, London's fashion scene is a vibrant tapestry of styles and influences. The city's Fashion Week is a major event on the global fashion calendar, showcasing the latest creations from both established and emerging designers.

Music is yet another domain where London's global influence is undeniable. From the iconic rock bands of the 1960s, like The Beatles and The Rolling Stones, to the contemporary grime artists of today, London has consistently produced music that resonates with global audiences. The city's music scene is as diverse as its population, encompassing genres ranging from classical to electronic, hip-hop to folk.

London's cultural diversity is one of its greatest assets. The city is a melting pot of cultures, languages, and cuisines. More than 300 languages are spoken in London, and the city's restaurants offer a culinary journey around the world. This diversity enriches London's cultural scene, fostering creativity and innovation.

However, London's global city status also brings challenges. The city's high cost of living and housing affordability crisis are pressing issues that affect many Londoners. Income inequality is another concern, with some boroughs experiencing significant levels of poverty.

Despite these challenges, London remains a magnet for people from all walks of life. The city's energy, diversity, and opportunities continue to attract talent and ambition from around the world. In the words of the London-based writer Ben Judah, "London is a city of dreams, a place where anything is possible."

In this book, we'll delve deeper into London's multifaceted identity as a global city. We'll explore its economic prowess, cultural vibrancy, political influence, and social challenges. We'll hear from Londoners themselves about their experiences and perspectives. And we'll consider what the future holds for this remarkable metropolis.

This chapter has served as an introduction to London's global city status, highlighting its influence in finance, culture, and beyond. As we move forward, we'll explore these themes in greater detail, painting a comprehensive picture of modern London in all its complexity and dynamism.

CHAPTER 2: FROM ROMAN LONDINIUM TO WORLD METROPOLIS

London wasn't built in a day. It wasn't even built in a century. The city's story is an epic saga spanning millennia, a tale of ambition, resilience, and constant reinvention. From a humble Roman trading post to a sprawling global metropolis, London's journey is a testament to the enduring power of human ingenuity and adaptability.

In the year 43 AD, Roman legions marched into what was then a marshy settlement on the banks of the River Thames. They named their new conquest Londinium, and thus began London's first chapter as a city. The Romans built a bustling trading port, complete with a forum, a basilica, and even a public bathhouse. Fragments of this Roman past can still be glimpsed in London today, from the remnants of the Roman wall that once encircled the city to the artifacts displayed in the Museum of London.

After the Romans departed in the 5th century, Londinium faced a period of decline. But the city's strategic location on the Thames made it too valuable to remain dormant for long. By the 11th century, London had re-emerged as a thriving centre of trade and commerce under the Saxons and later the Normans.

The Norman Conquest in 1066 marked a turning point in London's history. William the Conqueror, the new king of England, recognized the city's potential and set about transforming it into a royal capital. He built the Tower of London, a formidable fortress that still stands today, and Westminster Abbey, a grand church that would become the coronation site for English monarchs.

Over the following centuries, London continued to grow and evolve. The city weathered plagues, fires, and political upheavals, emerging each time stronger and more resilient. The Industrial Revolution of the 18th and 19th centuries brought a wave of economic and social change to London. The city became a global hub of manufacturing and trade, attracting migrants from across the country and the world.

The 20th century saw London face its greatest challenges yet. Two World Wars inflicted devastating damage on the city, but the Blitz spirit of resilience and defiance emerged as a defining characteristic of Londoners. In the post-war era, London rebuilt itself, embracing new styles of architecture and urban planning.

As the 20th century drew to a close, London underwent another transformation, this time driven by globalization and technological change. The city cemented its status as a global financial centre, attracting multinational corporations and financial institutions from around the world. The Canary Wharf development, a gleaming cluster of skyscrapers on the Isle of Dogs, became a symbol of London's new economic power.

Today, London is a city of contrasts and contradictions. It's a place where ancient history and cutting-edge technology coexist, where the traditions of the monarchy blend with the vibrant energy of a multicultural population. London's economy is among the most diverse of any city in the world, encompassing finance, technology, media, fashion, and the arts.

As historian Peter Ackroyd has noted, "London is a city that is always becoming, never being." This spirit of constant evolution is what makes London so unique and endlessly fascinating. The city's history is not just a collection of past events—it's a living legacy that continues to shape its present and future.

Looking ahead, London faces a number of challenges, including housing affordability, climate change, and social inequality. However, the city's history of resilience and reinvention suggests that it is well-equipped to meet these challenges head-on. As urbanist Richard Sennett has observed, "London is a city that knows how to change itself."

London's journey from Roman Londinium to global metropolis is a story of remarkable transformation and enduring spirit. It's a story that continues to unfold, with each new chapter adding to the rich tapestry of this extraordinary city.

CHAPTER 3: THE CITY OF LONDON: THE FINANCIAL HEART OF EUROPE

As the sun rises over London, a symphony of activity begins in the Square Mile, the historic heart of the city also known as the City of London. Here, in a maze of narrow streets and towering skyscrapers, the financial pulse of Europe beats. The City, as it's often referred to, is a global financial powerhouse, rivalling New York and Hong Kong in its influence and reach.

The City's significance in the global economy is undeniable. It's home to the London Stock Exchange, one of the world's oldest and largest stock exchanges, where trillions of pounds are traded each year. The City is also a major centre for banking, insurance, asset management, and legal services, attracting top talent from around the world.

To understand the City's impact, consider this: a decision made in a boardroom in the Square Mile can send shockwaves through global markets, impacting businesses and individuals across continents. The City's financial products and services are used by companies and governments worldwide, making it a vital cog in the machinery of the global economy.

"London is not just a financial centre, it's the financial centre," says Catherine McGuinness, former policy chair of the City of London Corporation. "It's the place where the world comes to

do business."
But the City isn't just about numbers and transactions. It's a place of ambition, innovation, and fierce competition. It's where fortunes are made and lost, where careers are launched and dreams are shattered. It's a place where the old and the new collide, where centuries-old traditions meet cutting-edge technology.

Take a walk through the City and you'll see this juxtaposition first-hand. Medieval churches nestled between glass-and-steel towers, cobblestone alleyways leading to bustling trading floors, historic pubs frequented by suited-up bankers. The City is a living museum of financial history, with each building and street corner whispering stories of past triumphs and failures. The City's success is due in part to its unique blend of tradition and innovation. The financial institutions that call the City home are steeped in history and tradition, yet they're also at the forefront of technological change. The City has embraced fintech, the use of technology to deliver financial services, and is home to a thriving community of fintech start-ups.

However, the City's dominance isn't without its challenges. Brexit, the UK's withdrawal from the European Union, has created uncertainty for the City's future. Some financial institutions have relocated operations to other European cities, and there are concerns about the City's ability to maintain its access to European markets.

The City is also grappling with issues of diversity and inclusion. While progress has been made, the financial sector remains predominantly male and white. There are ongoing efforts to increase representation of women and minorities in leadership positions.

Despite these challenges, the City remains a formidable force in the global economy. Its deep talent pool, robust infrastructure, and favourable regulatory environment continue to attract businesses and investment. The City is also adapting to the changing landscape of global finance, embracing new technologies and expanding its reach into emerging markets.

"The City is a resilient place," says McGuinness. "It's weathered many storms over the centuries and it will continue to do so. The City's future is bright, but it will require continued adaptation and innovation."

The City of London is more than just a financial district. It's a microcosm of the global economy, a place where the world's financial fortunes are shaped. It's a place of ambition, innovation, and constant change. As the financial heart of Europe, the City will continue to play a vital role in the years to come, shaping the global economy and impacting the lives of millions around the world.

CHAPTER 4: CROSSROADS OF CULTURES: LONDON'S DIVERSE DEMOGRAPHICS

Step onto the bustling streets of London, and you're not just in one city—you're in a world. A vibrant tapestry of languages, cuisines, and traditions unfurls before you, a testament to London's rich multicultural fabric. This diversity isn't just a demographic statistic; it's the lifeblood of the city, shaping its character, driving its creativity, and enriching its cultural landscape.

London's diversity is not a recent phenomenon. For centuries, the city has been a magnet for people from all corners of the globe. Waves of immigration, from the Huguenots fleeing religious persecution in the 17th century to the Windrush generation arriving from the Caribbean in the 1950s, have contributed to London's unique multicultural identity.

Today, London is one of the most diverse cities in the world. According to the 2021 census, over 37% of Londoners were born outside the UK, and more than 200 languages are spoken in the city. This diversity is reflected in every aspect of London life, from the food we eat to the music we listen to, the clothes we wear to the festivals we celebrate.

"London's diversity is its superpower," says Dr. Kavita Bhanot, a writer and academic who specializes in migration and diaspora studies. "It's what makes London so vibrant, so creative, so dynamic. It's what gives London its unique edge."

Take a stroll through Brixton Market, and you'll be transported to a Caribbean island, with the aroma of jerk chicken filling the air and reggae music pulsating from the stalls. Wander down Brick Lane, and you'll find yourself in the heart of London's Bangladeshi community, with curry houses lining the street and colourful saris on display. Head to Southall, and you'll be immersed in the sights and sounds of Punjabi culture, with bhangra music blasting from shops and Sikh temples adorned with vibrant decorations.

London's diversity isn't just about ethnic and cultural differences. The city is also home to a wide range of social and economic groups. From wealthy bankers in the City to working-class families in the East End, from bohemian artists in Shoreditch to tech entrepreneurs in Old Street, London is a city of many faces and voices.

This diversity is a source of strength, but it also presents challenges. London grapples with issues of inequality and social exclusion, with some communities feeling marginalized and left behind. The city's housing crisis is a major concern, with soaring rents and house prices making it difficult for many Londoners to afford a decent place to live.

Despite these challenges, London's diversity is ultimately a cause for celebration. It's a reminder that the city is a global hub, a place where people from all walks of life can come together and create something new. As writer Zadie Smith has put it, "London is a city built on the backs of immigrants. It's a city that thrives on difference."

London's multicultural fabric is woven into the very fabric of the city itself. It's in the architecture, the art, the music, the food, the language. It's in the way Londoners interact with each other, in the way they celebrate their differences and find common ground.

Looking ahead, London's diversity is only set to increase. The city is expected to continue to attract people from around the world, drawn by its economic opportunities, cultural vibrancy, and open-minded spirit. This influx of new arrivals will undoubtedly bring new challenges, but it will also enrich London's cultural landscape and ensure that the city remains a global crossroads of cultures.

London's diversity is not just a demographic fact; it's a lived reality. It's the stories of the people who call London home, the communities they create, and the contributions they make to the city's vibrant tapestry. It's the energy and creativity that flows from the city's multicultural melting pot. It's the heart and soul of London.

CHAPTER 5: LONDON'S TECH CITY: SILICON ROUNDABOUT AND BEYOND

The heart of London's tech scene beats not in a monolithic corporate campus but in a vibrant, ever-evolving ecosystem cantered around the Old Street Roundabout, affectionately nicknamed "Silicon Roundabout." This bustling intersection in East London has become synonymous with innovation, entrepreneurship, and the relentless pursuit of digital disruption. But London's tech scene extends far beyond this iconic landmark, encompassing a vast network of start-ups, scale-ups, investors, and talent that is reshaping the city's economic landscape.

London's rise as a global tech hub is a testament to its ability to adapt and reinvent itself. Once known primarily for its financial prowess, the city has embraced the digital age with open arms. Today, London is home to over 6,000 tech companies, employing over 300,000 people and generating billions in revenue. The city's tech scene is as diverse as its population, encompassing everything from fintech and e-commerce to artificial intelligence and medtech.

"London is a hotbed of tech talent," says Russ Shaw, founder of

Tech London Advocates, a network of tech leaders and experts. "We have world-class universities producing top graduates, a thriving start-up ecosystem, and a supportive government that recognizes the importance of tech to the economy."

The city's unique blend of history, culture, and diversity also plays a role in its tech success. London's rich heritage and global outlook attract talent from around the world, while its multiculturalism fosters a spirit of creativity and innovation.

The story of London's tech scene is one of rapid growth and transformation. In the early 2000s, a cluster of tech start-ups began to emerge around Old Street Roundabout, drawn by affordable rents, proximity to the City, and a burgeoning creative scene. This cluster quickly grew into a thriving ecosystem, attracting investment, talent, and media attention.

The government's decision to designate the area as "Tech City" in 2010 further fuelled its growth, providing support for start-ups and attracting global tech giants like Google and Amazon. Today, Tech City is a vibrant community of entrepreneurs, investors, and tech enthusiasts, with co-working spaces, accelerator programs, and networking events aplenty.

But London's tech scene isn't confined to Tech City. It's spread across the city, from the fintech hubs of Canary Wharf and Level39 to the creative tech clusters in Shoreditch and Hackney. The city's universities are also playing a key role, producing a steady stream of tech talent and fostering research and development.

London's tech scene is not without its challenges. The city's high cost of living and housing affordability crisis make it difficult for start-ups to attract and retain talent. Brexit has also created uncertainty for the tech sector, particularly around immigration and access to European markets.

However, London's tech scene remains resilient and optimistic. The city's strengths, including its talent pool, diverse economy, and global connectivity, continue to make it an attractive destination for tech companies. The government is also committed to supporting the sector, with initiatives like the Digital Skills Partnership and the Tech Nation visa scheme. "London's tech scene is still in its early stages," says Shaw. "There's so much potential for growth and innovation. I'm excited to see what the future holds for London as a global tech hub."

London's tech scene is a story of ambition, innovation, and the power of collaboration. It's a story that's still being written, with new chapters unfolding every day. As London continues to evolve and adapt to the digital age, its tech scene is poised to play an increasingly important role in the city's future.

CHAPTER 6: THE THAMES: LIFEBLOOD OF THE CAPITAL

The River Thames, a serpentine ribbon of water winding its way through the heart of London, is more than just a geographical feature. It's the city's lifeblood, a silent witness to centuries of history, a source of inspiration for artists and poets, and a vital artery for trade, transport, and recreation. To understand London, one must understand the Thames.

The river's influence on London's development is undeniable. It was the Thames that drew the Romans to this site in the 1st century AD, establishing Londinium as a key trading port. Throughout history, the Thames has shaped London's destiny, providing a vital link to the rest of the world and fuelling the city's economic and cultural growth.

"The Thames is London's greatest natural asset," says Sir Peter Bazalgette, Chair of the Thames Estuary Partnership. "It's the reason London exists. Without the Thames, London wouldn't be the city it is today."

The Thames has always been a working river. For centuries, it was a bustling highway of trade, with ships from around the world docking at its wharves and warehouses. The river's tidal nature made it ideal for transporting goods, and its banks were lined with industries that relied on its water for power and transportation.

The Industrial Revolution of the 18th and 19th centuries saw the Thames become even more central to London's economy. Factories and power plants sprang up along its banks, belching smoke and pollution into the air. The river became a symbol of both progress and industrial grime, a paradox that continues to resonate today.

In the 20th century, the Thames underwent a dramatic transformation. The decline of heavy industry and the rise of environmental awareness led to a clean-up of the river, and its banks were gradually transformed into public spaces and cultural attractions. Today, the Thames is a popular destination for tourists and locals alike, offering stunning views, riverside walks, and a variety of recreational activities.

The Thames is also a vital transport artery. The River Bus service ferries commuters and tourists up and down the river, offering a unique perspective on the city's iconic landmarks. The Thames Clippers, high-speed catamarans, provide a fast and efficient way to travel between central London and the O2 Arena in Greenwich.

But the Thames is more than just a transport route. It's a source of inspiration and recreation. The river's banks are dotted with parks and gardens, offering green oases in the heart of the city. The South Bank, home to the London Eye, the National Theatre, and the Tate Modern, is a cultural hub that attracts millions of visitors each year.

The Thames is also a source of artistic inspiration. Painters like J.M.W. Turner and Claude Monet captured its beauty on canvas, while writers like Charles Dickens and T.S. Eliot immortalized it in words. Today, the Thames continues to inspire artists, photographers, and filmmakers, who are drawn to its ever-changing moods and dramatic vistas.

However, the Thames faces challenges. Climate change and rising sea levels pose a threat to the city, and there are ongoing concerns about water quality and pollution. The Thames Tideway Tunnel, a major infrastructure project currently under construction, aims to tackle the problem of sewage overflow into the river.

Despite these challenges, the Thames remains a vital part of London's identity. It's a symbol of the city's history, its resilience, and its enduring spirit. As London continues to evolve and adapt to the challenges of the 21st century, the Thames will continue to play a central role in its future.

CHAPTER 7: LONDON'S GREEN SPACES: URBAN OASES IN A CONCRETE JUNGLE

Amidst the towering skyscrapers and bustling streets of London, a surprising tranquillity exists. London is a city of parks, a mosaic of green spaces that offer respite from the urban hustle and bustle. These verdant oases are not just a luxury; they are an essential part of London's urban fabric, playing a vital role in the city's well-being, sustainability, and overall quality of life.

London's green spaces are a testament to the city's commitment to preserving nature amidst the urban sprawl. With over 3,000 parks, gardens, and open spaces, London boasts more green space per capita than any other major city in the world. From the sprawling expanse of Richmond Park to the manicured lawns of St. James's Park, from the wildflower meadows of Hampstead Heath to the tranquil waters of Regent's Canal, London's green spaces offer something for everyone.

"London's parks are the city's lungs," says Tony Leach, CEO of the Royal Parks, the charity responsible for managing eight of London's most iconic parks. "They provide clean air, mitigate the effects of climate change, and offer a haven for wildlife. But they also provide a vital space for people to relax, exercise, and connect with nature."

The importance of green spaces in urban environments is well-documented. Research has shown that access to nature has a positive impact on physical and mental health, reducing stress, improving mood, and boosting creativity. Green spaces also play a crucial role in mitigating the effects of climate change, absorbing carbon dioxide, reducing air pollution, and regulating temperatures.

In London, green spaces are not just an amenity; they are a necessity. The city's dense population and high levels of pollution make access to nature all the more important. London's parks provide a vital escape from the urban grind, offering a place to breathe fresh air, exercise, and simply be.

London's green spaces are also a source of community and connection. They provide a place for people from all walks of life to come together, relax, and enjoy the outdoors. Parks host a wide range of events and activities, from outdoor concerts and festivals to sports leagues and community gardening projects. They are a melting pot of cultures and backgrounds, where people can interact, build relationships, and foster a sense of belonging.

The history of London's parks is a fascinating story of philanthropy, social reform, and visionary urban planning. In the 19th century, as London's population exploded, reformers like Octavia Hill recognized the need for green spaces to improve the health and well-being of the city's residents. Their efforts led to the creation of many of London's most beloved parks, including Victoria Park, Hampstead Heath, and Epping Forest.

Today, London's parks continue to evolve and adapt to the changing needs of the city. Many parks are undergoing renovations and upgrades to improve accessibility, create new facilities, and enhance biodiversity. The London National Park City initiative, launched in 2019, aims to make London the world's first National Park City, a place where people and nature can thrive together.

"The future of London is green," says Daniel Raven-Ellison, founder of the London National Park City. "We need to embrace nature as an integral part of our city, not just an afterthought. Our parks and green spaces are a precious resource that we need to protect and cherish for generations to come."

London's green spaces are a testament to the city's commitment to creating a sustainable and liveable urban environment. They are a source of pride, joy, and well-being for Londoners, and a model for other cities around the world. As London continues to grow and evolve, its green spaces will remain an essential part of its identity, providing a vital oasis in the heart of the urban jungle.

CHAPTER 8:
THE LONDON UNDERGROUND: PIONEERING URBAN TRANSPORTATION

The rumble of the train, the whoosh of air as it enters the station, the iconic roundel logo—these are the sensory hallmarks of the London Underground, or as it's affectionately known, the Tube. But this subterranean network is more than just a mode of transport; it's a symbol of London's ingenuity, resilience, and unwavering spirit. The Tube's history is intertwined with the city's growth, its challenges, and its triumphs. It's a story of engineering marvels, cultural icons, and the ever-evolving relationship between a city and its transport system.

The London Underground's genesis can be traced back to 1863, when the Metropolitan Railway opened, the world's first underground railway. This ground-breaking feat of engineering revolutionized urban transportation, offering a solution to London's burgeoning traffic congestion. The Tube quickly became an integral part of London life, ferrying commuters to work, shoppers to the West End, and tourists to iconic landmarks.

"The Tube is more than just a transport system," says Oliver

Green, Director of the London Transport Museum. "It's a social leveller, a cultural icon, and a symbol of London's modernity." The Tube's impact on London's development cannot be overstated. It opened up new areas of the city for development, spurred economic growth, and shaped the way Londoners lived and worked. The Tube's network expanded rapidly, reaching out to the suburbs and creating a vast interconnected web of lines and stations.

The Tube is also a cultural phenomenon. Its iconic map, designed by Harry Beck in 1933, is a masterpiece of graphic design, recognized around the world. The Tube's stations, with their distinctive architecture and tiling, are landmarks in their own right. The Tube has also been immortalized in literature, film, and music, becoming a symbol of London's identity.

But the Tube's influence extends far beyond London. It has served as a model for metro systems around the world. Cities like New York, Paris, and Tokyo have all borrowed from the Tube's design and operational principles. The Tube's emphasis on efficiency, safety, and accessibility has set a standard for urban transportation that is still emulated today.

"The London Underground is a pioneer in many aspects of metro development," says Professor John Preston, Director of the Centre for Transport Studies at University College London. "Its design, its technology, its operational practices—all have been influential in shaping metro systems around the world."

The Tube's influence can be seen in the layout of metro maps, the design of stations, and the use of technology to manage passenger flow and safety. The Tube's ticketing system, with its Oyster card and contactless payment options, has also been adopted by many other cities.

Despite its successes, the Tube faces challenges. The system is aging, with much of its infrastructure dating back to the Victorian era. Overcrowding is a persistent problem, particularly during peak hours. The Tube's fares are also among the highest in the world, making it a financial burden for many Londoners.

However, the Tube is not standing still. It's undergoing a major modernization program, with new trains, signalling systems, and station upgrades being rolled out. The Elizabeth line, a new cross-London railway line, opened in 2022,providing much-needed capacity and improving connectivity across the city.

"The Tube is constantly evolving," says Green. "It's a dynamic system that adapts to the changing needs of Londoners. The challenges are real, but the Tube has a proven track record of innovation and resilience."

The London Underground is more than just a transport system. It's a symbol of London's ingenuity, resilience, and global influence. It's a story of engineering marvels, cultural icons, and the ever-evolving relationship between a city and its transport system. As London continues to grow and change, the Tube will remain an integral part of its identity, a testament to the city's enduring spirit and its ability to innovate and adapt.

CHAPTER 9: FROM THE GLOBE TO THE WEST END: LONDON AS A THEATRE CAPITAL

The lights dim, the curtain rises, and a hush falls over the audience as a world of drama, music, and spectacle unfolds on the stage. This is the magic of London's theatre scene, a vibrant and diverse landscape that encompasses everything from Shakespearean classics to cutting-edge experimental works. London's theatrical heritage is rich and deep, dating back to the Elizabethan era, and its current status as a global theatre capital is undeniable.

The story of London theatre is inextricably linked to the Globe Theatre, the iconic open-air playhouse where William Shakespeare's works were first performed. Built in 1599, the Globe was a cultural hub, attracting audiences from all walks of life. Shakespeare's plays, with their universal themes of love, loss, ambition, and betrayal, resonated with audiences then as they do now. The Globe's legacy lives on in the reconstructed Shakespeare's Globe, a faithful replica that hosts performances of Shakespeare's plays and other historical dramas.

"The Globe is a symbol of London's theatrical heritage," says Farah Karim-Cooper, Co-Director of Education at

Shakespeare's Globe. "It's a reminder of the power of theatre to entertain, educate, and inspire."

As London grew and prospered, so did its theatre scene. The West End, with its grand theatres and dazzling productions, became the epicentre of London's theatrical life. It's home to long-running musicals like "The Phantom of the Opera" and "Les Misérables," as well as new plays and revivals of classics. The West End is a major tourist attraction, drawing millions of visitors each year.

But London's theatre scene is not confined to the West End. There are countless smaller theatres scattered throughout the city, offering a diverse range of productions. The National Theatre, the Royal Court Theatre, and the Young Vic are just a few of the institutions that nurture new talent and push the boundaries of theatrical form.

"London's theatre scene is incredibly diverse," says Rufus Norris, Artistic Director of the National Theatre. "There's something for everyone, from big-budget musicals to experimental theatre, from Shakespeare to new writing."

London's theatre scene is also a reflection of the city's multiculturalism. Theatres like the Tara Arts and the Bush Theatre showcase work by artists from diverse backgrounds, exploring themes of identity, migration, and social justice. The annual London International Festival of Theatre (LIFT) brings together artists from around the world, offering a global perspective on contemporary theatre.

London's theatre scene is not without its challenges. The high cost of production and ticket prices can make theatre inaccessible to some audiences. The COVID-19 pandemic had a devastating impact on the theatre industry, forcing many theatres to close temporarily.

However, London's theatre scene is resilient. Theatres have adapted to the challenges, finding new ways to connect with audiences through online performances and outdoor productions. The government has provided financial support to help theatres recover from the pandemic.

Looking ahead, London's theatre scene is poised for a renaissance. New theatres are opening, and established theatres are expanding their programming. The city's diverse population and global outlook ensure a constant flow of new ideas and talent. As technology continues to evolve, theatre will find new ways to engage audiences and tell stories.

"The future of London theatre is bright," says Norris. "There's a new generation of artists and audiences who are passionate about theatre. We need to nurture that passion and ensure that theatre remains a vital part of London's cultural landscape."

London's theatre scene is a vibrant and dynamic ecosystem, a testament to the city's rich heritage and its enduring love of the performing arts. From the Globe to the West End, from Shakespeare to cutting-edge new works, London's theatres offer a world of stories, emotions, and experiences. The magic of London theatre is waiting to be discovered.

CHAPTER 10:
SEATS OF POWER:
WESTMINSTER
AND MODERN
BRITISH POLITICS

The Gothic spires of Westminster Abbey pierce the London skyline, a constant reminder of the city's deep-rooted history and enduring power. Nestled alongside the abbey is the Palace of Westminster, the seat of the UK Parliament and the beating heart of British politics. Within these hallowed halls, decisions are made that resonate throughout the nation and reverberate around the world. London's role as the epicentre of UK political life is undeniable, shaped by centuries of tradition, power struggles, and democratic evolution.

The Palace of Westminster, often simply referred to as Westminster, is a symbol of Britain's parliamentary democracy. It's where the House of Commons and the House of Lords meet to debate and legislate, where Prime Ministers rise and fall, and where the fate of the nation is often decided. The Palace's history is intertwined with that of the UK itself, a testament to the country's long and often tumultuous journey towards democracy.

"Westminster is more than just a building," says Professor Meg Russell, Director of the Constitution Unit at University

College London. "It's the embodiment of British democracy, a place where the voices of the people are represented and where power is held to account."

Westminster's influence extends far beyond its walls. The decisions made in the Palace of Westminster affect every aspect of British life, from healthcare and education to defence and foreign policy. The Prime Minister, who resides at 10 Downing Street, just a stone's throw from the Palace of Westminster, is the head of the UK government and wields immense power.

But Westminster is not the only seat of power in London. The city is also home to a vast network of government departments, agencies, and quangos, each playing a role in the machinery of government. Whitehall, the street that runs from Parliament Square to Trafalgar Square, is synonymous with the British civil service, the engine room of government.

London's role as the political capital of the UK is not without its critics. Some argue that Westminster is too remote from the concerns of ordinary people, that it's dominated by a political elite who are out of touch with the realities of life outside London. There are also concerns about the concentration of power in London, with some regions feeling marginalized and neglected.

"The perception of London as the centre of power can create resentment in other parts of the country," says Professor Michael Kenny, Director of the Bennett Institute for Public Policy at the University of Cambridge. "There's a feeling that decisions are being made by people who don't understand or care about the challenges faced by people outside London."

The Brexit referendum of 2016 exposed these divisions, with a majority of voters outside London opting to leave the European Union while London voted to remain. This result highlighted the growing disconnect between London and the rest of the country, a disconnect that has fuelled calls for greater devolution of power to the regions.

Despite these challenges, London's role as the political

capital of the UK is unlikely to change anytime soon. The city's history, its infrastructure, and its concentration of expertise make it the natural home for the UK government. However, there are ongoing efforts to make Westminster more representative and responsive to the needs of the entire country.

The House of Lords, the upper chamber of Parliament, is undergoing reforms to make it more democratic and diverse. The government is also exploring ways to decentralize power, giving more autonomy to local and regional authorities.

"Westminster needs to evolve if it wants to remain relevant in the 21st century," says Russell. "It needs to become more inclusive, more transparent, and more responsive to the needs of the whole country."

London's role as the centre of UK political life is a complex and multifaceted issue. It's a story of power, tradition, and democratic evolution. It's a story of challenges and opportunities, of divisions and unity. As the UK navigates the uncharted waters of Brexit and grapples with the challenges of the 21st century, London's role as the seat of power will continue to be a subject of debate and discussion.

CHAPTER 11: THE LONDON SCHOOL OF ECONOMICS AND POLITICAL SCIENCE: SHAPING GLOBAL THOUGHT

In a quiet corner of London's bustling Aldwych, a grand Edwardian building stands as a beacon of intellectual inquiry and social progress. This is the London School of Economics and Political Science (LSE), an institution that has been shaping global thought for over a century. From its humble beginnings as a night school for working men and women, the LSE has grown into a world-renowned centre for research and teaching in the social sciences, attracting students and faculty from around the globe.

The LSE's influence on world affairs is undeniable. Its alumni include heads of state, Nobel laureates, business leaders, and social activists who have shaped the course of history. The school's research has informed policy debates on everything from poverty and inequality to climate change and global governance.

"The LSE is a global institution with a global impact," says

Baroness Minouche Shafik, Director of the LSE. "Our mission is to understand the causes of things, to make the world a better place, and to educate the next generation of leaders."

The LSE's impact stems from its unique approach to education and research. The school is renowned for its rigorous academic standards, its emphasis on interdisciplinary learning, and its commitment to social engagement. LSE students are encouraged to think critically, challenge conventional wisdom, and engage with the real world.

The LSE's faculty is a who's who of social science luminaries. Nobel laureates like Paul Krugman and Christopher Pissarides have taught at the LSE, and its current faculty includes leading experts in economics, political science, sociology, anthropology, and law.

The LSE's research is at the forefront of social science inquiry. The school's research centres and institutes tackle some of the most pressing challenges facing the world today, from climate change and global inequality to financial instability and political conflict. The LSE's research is not just theoretical; it's designed to have a real-world impact, informing policy debates and shaping public discourse.

But the LSE's influence extends far beyond its research and teaching. The school is a vibrant hub of intellectual and cultural activity, hosting public lectures, debates, and conferences that attract leading thinkers from around the world. The LSE's alumni network is a powerful force, with graduates occupying positions of influence in governments, businesses, and NGOs worldwide.

"The LSE is a community of people who are passionate about making a difference in the world," says Shafik. "Our alumni are our greatest ambassadors, and they are making a real impact in every field imaginable."

The LSE's impact can be seen in the policies of governments, the strategies of businesses, and the work of NGOs. The school's graduates have gone on to lead countries, shape economic policy, and fight for social justice.

The LSE's influence is not without its critics. Some accuse the school of being too closely aligned with the political and economic establishment, of promoting a neoliberal agenda that favours deregulation and free markets. Others criticize the school for its high tuition fees, which can make it inaccessible to students from disadvantaged backgrounds.

Despite these criticisms, the LSE remains a powerful force in shaping global thought. Its commitment to academic excellence, social engagement, and interdisciplinary learning continues to attract the brightest minds from around the world. As the world faces new and complex challenges in the 21st century, the LSE's role in shaping global thought will only become more important.

CHAPTER 12: THE BRITISH MUSEUM: PRESERVING WORLD HERITAGE IN THE HEART OF LONDON

In the heart of London, a grand neoclassical edifice houses a treasure trove of human history. The British Museum, with its iconic colonnaded façade, is not just a repository of artifacts, but a microcosm of the world's cultures, a testament to human creativity, ingenuity, and interconnectedness. Yet, the museum's vast collection, amassed over centuries of exploration, conquest, and trade, is also a source of controversy, raising complex questions about colonialism, cultural heritage, and restitution.

Founded in 1753, the British Museum is one of the oldest and largest museums in the world, with a collection of over eight million objects spanning two million years of human history. Its galleries house iconic artifacts like the Rosetta Stone, the Parthenon Sculptures (also known as the Elgin Marbles), and the Egyptian mummies, drawing millions of visitors each year. "The British Museum is a unique institution," says Dr. Hartwig Fischer, its Director. "It's a place where people from all over the world can come together to explore the richness and diversity of human cultures."

The museum's role in preserving world heritage is undeniable. Its vast collection, meticulously catalogued and curated, provides a window into the past, offering insights into ancient civilizations, artistic traditions, and scientific discoveries. The museum's educational programs and exhibitions reach a global audience, fostering understanding and appreciation of different cultures.

However, the museum's collection is also a subject of intense debate. Many of its most prized artifacts were acquired during the era of British colonialism, often under questionable circumstances. The Parthenon Sculptures, for example, were removed from Greece by Lord Elgin in the early 19th century, and their rightful ownership remains a contentious issue.

"The British Museum is a product of its time," says Professor Dan Hicks, Curator at the Pitt Rivers Museum in Oxford. "It's a legacy of colonialism, and its collection reflects that history. We need to acknowledge this context and engage in a critical dialogue about the ethics of collecting and displaying cultural heritage."

The debate over restitution, the return of cultural artifacts to their countries of origin, has intensified in recent years. Many countries, including Greece, Nigeria, and Egypt, have demanded the return of artifacts that they believe were taken illegally or under duress. The British Museum has resisted these calls, arguing that it is a universal museum with a responsibility to preserve and share world heritage for the benefit of all.

"The British Museum is a global museum for the world," says Fischer. "Our collection belongs to everyone, and it's our duty to make it accessible to as many people as possible."

The debate over the British Museum's collection is not just about legal and ethical issues. It's also about identity, memory, and cultural heritage. For many countries, their cultural artifacts are not just objects; they are symbols of their national identity and a source of pride and inspiration.

"The Parthenon Sculptures are not just pieces of marble," says

Dr. Elena Korka, Director of the Acropolis Museum in Athens. "They are part of our cultural DNA. They belong in Greece, where they can be seen in their proper context."

The British Museum is at a crossroads. It must find a way to reconcile its colonial past with its present-day mission of preserving and sharing world heritage. This will require a willingness to engage in open and honest dialogue with source communities, to acknowledge the injustices of the past, and to explore new models of collaboration and shared ownership.

The British Museum is a microcosm of the challenges and opportunities facing museums in the 21st century. As globalization and decolonization reshape our understanding of culture and heritage, museums must adapt to a new era of transparency, accountability, and inclusivity.

The British Museum's story is far from over. It is a story that continues to unfold, with new chapters being written every day. As the museum navigates the complex issues of colonialism, cultural heritage, and restitution, it has the opportunity to redefine its role in the 21st century and to become a model for museums around the world.

CHAPTER 13: LONDON FASHION WEEK: SETTING GLOBAL TRENDS

The energy is palpable, the anticipation electric. Flashing cameras illuminate a runway pulsating with models showcasing avant-garde designs. This is London Fashion Week (LFW), a biannual spectacle where creativity and commerce collide, setting the stage for global fashion trends. It's a showcase of London's unique position as a fashion capital, a melting pot of cultures, styles, and influences that consistently pushes the boundaries of fashion innovation.

London's fashion scene is a vibrant tapestry woven from threads of history, diversity, and rebellion. From the punk movement's DIY ethos to the avant-garde creations of Alexander McQueen, London has always been a city that embraces individuality and challenges the status quo. This spirit of innovation is evident in every aspect of LFW, from the emerging designers showcasing their collections to the established brands pushing the boundaries of creativity.

"London Fashion Week is a platform for creative expression," says Caroline Rush, Chief Executive of the British Fashion Council, the organization behind LFW. "It's a place where designers can showcase their unique vision and challenge the norms of the industry."

LFW's influence on the global fashion scene is undeniable. The event attracts buyers, journalists, and influencers from around the world, eager to discover the latest trends and emerging talent. The collections showcased at LFW often set the tone for the upcoming season, influencing everything from high-street fashion to couture.

London's fashion industry is a significant contributor to the UK economy, generating billions of pounds in revenue each year. LFW itself is estimated to contribute over £300 million to the UK economy, through tourism, retail sales, and media coverage.

But LFW is not just about economic impact. It's also a cultural phenomenon, a celebration of creativity and diversity. The event showcases a wide range of designers, from established names like Vivienne Westwood and Burberry to emerging talents like Richard Quinn and Molly Goddard. LFW is also a platform for diversity and inclusion, with designers from different backgrounds and cultures showcasing their work.

"London Fashion Week is a reflection of London itself," says Rush. "It's a diverse and inclusive city, and that's reflected in the diversity of designers and collections we see at LFW."

The COVID-19 pandemic has had a profound impact on the fashion industry, and LFW has not been immune. The event was forced to go virtual in 2020 and 2021, but it has since returned to a physical format, albeit with some changes. The pandemic has accelerated the shift towards digital platforms, with many designers now showcasing their collections online as well as on the runway.

"The pandemic has forced the fashion industry to adapt and innovate," says Rush. "We're seeing new ways of presenting collections, new ways of engaging with audiences, and new ways of thinking about the future of fashion."

Despite the challenges, London's fashion scene remains vibrant and resilient. The city's designers continue to push the boundaries of creativity, and LFW continues to attract a global audience. London's fashion industry is also embracing sustainability, with many designers adopting eco-friendly practices and materials.

"The future of fashion is sustainable," says Rush. "We need to create a fashion industry that is not only creative and innovative, but also responsible and ethical."

London Fashion Week is a testament to the city's enduring influence on the global fashion scene. It's a showcase of creativity, diversity, and innovation, a platform for emerging talent and a catalyst for change. As London continues to evolve and adapt to the challenges of the 21st century, its fashion scene will remain a vibrant and influential force, shaping the future of fashion around the world.

CHAPTER 14: THE BBC AND LONDON'S MEDIA LANDSCAPE

The iconic chimes of Big Ben, resonating from the Elizabeth Tower at the Palace of Westminster, are synonymous with London. But another London institution, often considered a voice of the nation and a beacon of global journalism, is the British Broadcasting Corporation, better known as the BBC. Housed in the sleek, modern Broadcasting House, just a stone's throw from Oxford Street's bustling retail haven, the BBC is a testament to London's pivotal role in shaping the global media landscape.

London's influence on media and journalism dates back centuries. The city's first newspapers emerged in the 17th century, providing a platform for political discourse and social commentary. In the 19th century, London became a hub for international news agencies, reporting on events from around the world. The advent of radio and television in the 20th century further cemented London's status as a media powerhouse.

Today, London is a global media capital, home to a diverse array of media outlets, from traditional newspapers and broadcasters to digital news start-ups and social media influencers. The city's media landscape is a reflection of its multiculturalism, with outlets catering to a wide range of audiences and interests.

"London is a global media hub," says Fran Unsworth, former Director of News and Current Affairs at the BBC. "It's a place where ideas are generated, stories are told, and opinions are shaped. The city's diversity and openness make it an ideal environment for media innovation and experimentation."

The BBC, founded in 1922, is the crown jewel of London's media landscape. As a public service broadcaster, the BBC has a unique mandate to inform, educate, and entertain. Its news and current affairs programs are watched and listened to by millions around the world, setting a standard for journalistic integrity and impartiality.

"The BBC is a global institution," says Unsworth. "It's a trusted source of news and information, and it plays a vital role in promoting understanding and dialogue across cultures."

The BBC's influence extends far beyond its news output. Its dramas, documentaries, and comedies are enjoyed by global audiences, showcasing British talent and creativity. The BBC's natural history documentaries, such as "Planet Earth" and "Blue Planet," have raised awareness of environmental issues and inspired a new generation of conservationists.

But the BBC is not without its critics. Some accuse it of having a left-wing bias, while others criticize its funding model, which is based on a mandatory license fee paid by all TV-owning households in the UK. The rise of digital media and streaming services has also challenged the BBC's dominance, forcing it to adapt to a new era of competition and changing audience habits.

"The BBC is facing a period of unprecedented change," says Unsworth. "But it's a resilient organization, and it will continue to adapt and innovate to meet the challenges of the digital age."

London's media landscape is not just about the BBC. The city is home to a thriving newspaper industry, with titles like The Times, The Guardian, and The Financial Times enjoying global reputations. London is also a major centre for magazine publishing, with titles like Vogue, GQ, and The Economist reaching a global readership.

The rise of digital media has transformed London's media landscape. Online news outlets like The Independent and BuzzFeed have disrupted the traditional newspaper industry, while social media platforms like Twitter and Facebook have given a voice to citizen journalists and activists.

"The digital revolution has democratized the media," says Emily Bell, Director of the Tow Centre for Digital Journalism at Columbia University. "It's given a voice to people who were previously excluded from the mainstream media, and it's created new opportunities for innovation and experimentation."

London's media landscape is a dynamic and ever-evolving ecosystem. It's a place where tradition and innovation collide, where global perspectives meet local voices, and where the power of storytelling is harnessed to inform, educate, and entertain. London's role in shaping global media and journalism is undeniable, and its influence is set to continue in the digital age.

CHAPTER 15: LONDON'S AIRPORTS: GATEWAYS TO THE WORLD

The roar of jet engines, the symphony of languages, the anticipation of arrivals and departures—these are the sounds and sights that define London's airports, bustling gateways to the world. As a global transportation hub, London's airports play a pivotal role in connecting the UK to the rest of the world, facilitating trade, tourism, and cultural exchange. Their impact extends far beyond the aviation industry, shaping the city's economy, infrastructure, and international standing.

London boasts six major airports: Heathrow, Gatwick, Stansted, Luton, City, and Southend. Each airport has its own distinct character and role, catering to different types of travellers and airlines. Heathrow, the busiest airport in Europe, is a global hub for long-haul flights, connecting London to major cities around the world. Gatwick, the second busiest airport, is a popular choice for leisure travellers, offering a wide range of flights to European destinations. Stansted, Luton, and Southend are primarily used by low-cost carriers, offering affordable flights to a growing number of destinations. City Airport, located in the heart of London's financial district, caters to business travellers, offering quick and convenient access to the city centre.

"London's airports are a vital part of the city's infrastructure," says Tim Alderslade, Chief Executive of Airlines UK, the trade association for UK-registered airlines. "They connect London to the world, enabling trade, tourism, and cultural exchange. They are also major employers, providing thousands of jobs and contributing billions of pounds to the UK economy."

The economic impact of London's airports is significant. In 2019, the airports generated over £19 billion in economic activity and supported over 375,000 jobs. Heathrow alone contributes over £12 billion to the UK economy and supports over 114,000 jobs.

But the airports' impact goes beyond economics. They are gateways to the world, facilitating the movement of people, goods, and ideas. London's airports are a microcosm of the city's diversity, with passengers from all corners of the globe passing through their terminals. The airports also play a role in cultural exchange, with art exhibitions, cultural events, and performances often taking place in their public spaces.

"London's airports are more than just transportation hubs," says Alderslade. "They are cultural spaces, community hubs, and economic engines. They are a reflection of London's global outlook and its commitment to connectivity."

However, London's airports also face challenges. The COVID-19 pandemic had a devastating impact on the aviation industry, causing a sharp decline in passenger numbers and revenue. The airports have been slow to recover, with travel restrictions and concerns about new variants of the virus continuing to dampen demand.

The airports are also grappling with environmental concerns. The aviation industry is a major source of greenhouse gas emissions, and there is growing pressure to reduce the sector's carbon footprint. London's airports are investing in new technologies and operational practices to reduce their environmental impact, but more needs to be done to achieve net zero emissions.

Another challenge facing London's airports is capacity constraints. Heathrow, in particular, is operating at near capacity, and there are ongoing debates about the need for a third runway. The expansion of Heathrow is a controversial issue, with opponents citing concerns about noise pollution, air quality, and climate change.

Despite these challenges, London's airports remain a vital part of the city's infrastructure and its global connectivity. The airports are adapting to the changing landscape of air travel, embracing new technologies and sustainable practices. As the world emerges from the pandemic, London's airports are poised to play a key role in the recovery of the aviation industry and the reconnection of people and places around the world.

CHAPTER 16: THE LONDON STOCK EXCHANGE: PULSE OF THE GLOBAL ECONOMY

In the heart of the City of London, amidst the towering skyscrapers and historic landmarks, lies an institution that embodies the relentless dynamism of global finance: The London Stock Exchange (LSE). As the oldest stock exchange in the world, its history is a captivating narrative of economic evolution, technological innovation, and the unwavering pursuit of capital. The LSE's role in international finance is monumental, influencing financial markets worldwide and shaping the fortunes of countless individuals and corporations.

Since its inception in 1698, the LSE has been a central pillar of the global economy. From the early days of trading shares in coffee houses to the modern era of electronic trading, the LSE has continuously adapted to the changing tides of finance. It has witnessed the rise and fall of empires, the booms and busts of markets, and the transformative power of technology.

"The London Stock Exchange is a microcosm of the global economy," says Julia Hoggett, CEO of the London Stock Exchange plc. "It's a place where the world's financial fortunes are shaped, where companies raise capital to fuel their growth, and where investors seek opportunities to build wealth."

The LSE's impact on the global economy is profound. It provides a platform for companies from around the world to raise capital by listing their shares on the exchange. This access to capital allows companies to invest in growth, create jobs, and drive innovation. The LSE also offers a wide range of financial products and services, including trading in equities, bonds, derivatives, and exchange-traded funds (ETFs). These products and services are used by investors, businesses, and governments worldwide, making the LSE a vital cog in the machinery of the global economy.

"The London Stock Exchange is a global marketplace," says Hoggett. "It connects investors and companies from around the world, facilitating the flow of capital and enabling businesses to grow and thrive."

The LSE's influence extends beyond its role as a marketplace. It also plays a crucial role in setting standards and regulations for the financial industry. The exchange's rules and procedures are designed to ensure fair and transparent trading, protect investors, and maintain market integrity. The LSE also works closely with regulators and policymakers to promote stability and resilience in the financial system.

However, the LSE's prominence is not without its challenges. Brexit, the UK's withdrawal from the European Union, has created uncertainty for the London financial market. Some financial institutions have relocated operations to other European cities, and there are concerns about the LSE's ability to maintain its status as a leading global financial centre.

The rise of new technologies, such as blockchain and artificial intelligence, is also disrupting the financial industry, forcing traditional exchanges like the LSE to adapt and innovate. The LSE has embraced these technologies, launching new platforms and services that leverage the power of data and analytics to provide investors with greater insights and transparency.

"The LSE is committed to embracing new technologies and adapting to the changing landscape of global finance," says Hoggett. "We believe that innovation is key to our continued success and our ability to serve our customers and stakeholders."

Despite the challenges, the LSE remains a formidable force in international finance. Its long history, deep liquidity, and diverse range of products and services make it an attractive destination for investors and companies from around the world. The LSE's commitment to innovation and its focus on sustainability are positioning it for continued success in the years to come.

The London Stock Exchange is more than just a marketplace. It's a symbol of London's financial prowess, a testament to the city's enduring spirit of innovation and resilience. As the global economy continues to evolve, the LSE will remain a vital player, shaping the future of finance and influencing the fortunes of individuals and corporations worldwide.

CHAPTER 17: MULTICULTURAL CUISINES: LONDON AS A GLOBAL FOOD CAPITAL

The aroma of freshly baked bagels wafts from a Brick Lane bakery, the sizzle of jerk chicken fills Brixton Market, and the tantalizing scent of aromatic spices emanates from a Southall curry house. These sensory delights are just a taste of London's diverse culinary scene, a gastronomic melting pot that reflects the city's rich multicultural tapestry. From Michelin-starred restaurants to bustling street food markets, London's food scene is a culinary adventure that caters to every palate and budget.

London's diversity has been a driving force behind its culinary evolution. Waves of immigration have brought with them a rich array of culinary traditions, ingredients, and techniques. From the Huguenots who introduced French cuisine to the city in the 17th century to the Windrush generation who brought Caribbean flavours in the 20th century, each wave of migration has left its mark on London's food scene.

"London's culinary scene is a reflection of its history," says food writer and historian Bee Wilson. "It's a living testament to the city's openness to new cultures and ideas."

Today, London is a global food capital, rivalling cities like New York, Tokyo, and Paris in its diversity and quality of cuisine. The city boasts over 18,000 restaurants, offering a culinary journey around the world. You can savour authentic Chinese dim sum in Chinatown, indulge in fragrant Indian curries in Southall, sample spicy Thai noodles in Soho, or savour traditional Italian pasta in Clerkenwell.

The rise of street food markets has further democratized London's food scene. Markets like Borough Market, Maltby Street Market, and Broadway Market offer a diverse range of affordable and delicious food from around the world. These markets have become social hubs, where people from all walks of life come together to eat, drink, and socialize.

"Street food markets have revolutionized the way Londoners eat," says food blogger and market enthusiast Kerstin Rodgers. "They've made it possible to sample a wide range of cuisines without breaking the bank. They've also created a sense of community and excitement around food."

London's culinary diversity is not just about ethnic cuisine. The city is also home to a thriving modern British food scene, which draws inspiration from both traditional British dishes and global culinary influences. Chefs like Fergus Henderson and Yotam Ottolenghi have championed seasonal, locally sourced ingredients and innovative cooking techniques, creating a new wave of British cuisine that is both exciting and accessible.

"London's food scene is constantly evolving," says Jay Rayner, restaurant critic for The Observer. "There's a new generation of chefs who are pushing the boundaries of what British food can be. They're taking inspiration from the city's diversity and creating dishes that are both delicious and surprising."

However, London's food scene is not without its challenges. The high cost of living and operating a restaurant in London can make it difficult for small businesses to survive. The COVID-19 pandemic has also had a devastating impact on the hospitality industry, with many restaurants forced to close their doors.

Despite these challenges, London's food scene remains resilient and innovative. Restaurants have adapted to the pandemic by offering takeaway and delivery services, and many have embraced outdoor dining. The city's diverse population and global outlook ensure a constant flow of new culinary ideas and trends.

"London's food scene is a testament to the city's resilience and creativity," says Wilson. "It's a place where people from all over the world come together to share their food and their culture. It's a truly global culinary capital."

London's culinary landscape is a reflection of its rich history, its diverse population, and its open-minded spirit. It's a place where culinary traditions from around the world come together to create something new and exciting. London's food scene is a feast for the senses, a culinary adventure that is sure to leave a lasting impression on any visitor.

CHAPTER 18: THE ROYAL FAMILY: LONDON'S MONARCHICAL HERITAGE IN THE MODERN ERA

In an age of rapid change and technological advancement, London holds onto a tradition that links it to its storied past: the monarchy. The Royal Family, with its palaces, ceremonies, and enduring symbolism, plays a multifaceted role in shaping London's global image. It is a unique blend of history, culture, and political influence, attracting worldwide fascination and contributing significantly to London's allure.

At the heart of this regal presence is Buckingham Palace, the Queen's official residence and a symbol of the monarchy's power and prestige. The Changing of the Guard ceremony, a daily spectacle of precision and pageantry, draws crowds of tourists and locals alike. Other royal residences, such as Kensington Palace, Windsor Castle, and the Tower of London, add to the city's royal tapestry, each with its own rich history and cultural significance.

"The monarchy is an intrinsic part of London's identity," says

Dr. Anna Whitelock, a historian and author specializing in the modern monarchy. "It's a living link to the past, a source of national pride, and a symbol of stability and continuity."

The monarchy's impact on London's global image is undeniable. It's a powerful brand that attracts tourists, investors, and talent from around the world. Royal events, such as weddings, jubilees, and state visits, generate significant media attention and boost the city's economy. A 2017 report estimated that the Royal Family's contribution to UK tourism was worth over £550 million annually.

"The monarchy is a unique asset for London," says Patricia Yates, Director of Strategy and Communications at VisitBritain, the national tourism agency. "It's a major draw for visitors from around the world, and it helps to promote Britain as a destination for heritage and culture."

Beyond tourism, the monarchy also plays a role in shaping London's cultural and social landscape. Royal patronage of arts organizations, charities, and educational institutions lends prestige and support to these endeavors. The Royal Family's charitable work, particularly in areas like conservation and youth development, has a positive impact on communities across London and the UK.

However, the monarchy's role in modern London is not without its complexities and controversies. Some argue that it is an outdated institution, a relic of a bygone era that has no place in a modern democracy. Others criticize the cost of maintaining the monarchy, particularly in a time of economic hardship.

"The monarchy is a symbol of privilege and inequality," says Graham Smith, CEO of Republic, an organization that campaigns for the abolition of the monarchy. "It's an undemocratic institution that has no place in a modern society."

The debate over the monarchy's future is ongoing, with opinions ranging from ardent support to calls for its abolition. However, it is undeniable that the monarchy remains a significant part of London's identity and its global image. The recent passing of Queen Elizabeth II and the accession of King Charles III have sparked renewed interest in the monarchy, both in the UK and around the world.

"The monarchy is at a crossroads," says Whitelock. "It needs to adapt to the changing times and find new ways to connect with a younger and more diverse audience. But its enduring appeal is undeniable, and it will continue to play a role in shaping London's global image for many years to come."

The Royal Family's presence in London is a unique blend of tradition, modernity, and global influence. It's a symbol of the city's rich history, its cultural vibrancy, and its enduring appeal. Whether one views the monarchy with admiration or scepticism, its impact on London's global image is undeniable. As the city continues to evolve and adapt to the challenges of the 21st century, the monarchy will remain a fascinating and contentious subject, a source of both pride and debate for Londoners and the world.

CHAPTER 19: LONDON'S UNIVERSITIES: NURTURING GLOBAL TALENT

Within the labyrinthine streets of London, a vibrant intellectual ecosystem thrives, attracting the brightest minds from across the globe. The city boasts a constellation of world-renowned universities, each a unique hub of learning, research, and innovation. These institutions not only shape the future of their students but also contribute significantly to London's global influence and intellectual vibrancy.

London's universities, with their rich histories and diverse offerings, cater to a wide range of academic interests and career aspirations. From the centuries-old traditions of the University of Oxford and the University of Cambridge to the modern campuses of Imperial College London and University College London (UCL), the city offers a unique blend of academic rigor and cutting-edge research.

"London is an unparalleled hub for higher education," says Professor Wendy Thomson, Vice-Chancellor of the University of London. "The city's diversity, cultural richness, and global outlook create an ideal environment for students and scholars from all over the world."

London's universities are not just academic institutions; they are economic powerhouses, cultural centres, and incubators for innovation. They contribute billions of pounds to the UK economy each year, generating employment, attracting investment, and driving research and development. The universities also play a crucial role in London's cultural landscape, hosting public lectures, exhibitions, and performances that enrich the city's intellectual life.

"London's universities are integral to the city's identity," says Thomson. "They are a source of pride, a magnet for talent, and a catalyst for innovation. They are a testament to London's commitment to education, research, and the pursuit of knowledge."

The international appeal of London's universities is undeniable. According to the Higher Education Statistics Agency, over 200,000 international students were enrolled in London's universities in the 2021-2022 academic year, making it one of the most popular destinations for international students in the world. These students bring with them a diversity of perspectives, experiences, and cultures, enriching the learning environment and fostering global understanding.

"London's universities are truly global institutions," says Dr. Tim Gore, Director of the Institute for Global Affairs at the London School of Economics and Political Science (LSE). "Our students come from over 150 countries, and our faculty represent a wide range of nationalities and backgrounds. This diversity is a strength, enabling us to tackle global challenges from multiple perspectives."

The benefits of international education are numerous. For students, it offers the opportunity to broaden their horizons, gain new perspectives, and develop intercultural skills that are increasingly valuable in a globalized world. For universities, international students bring diversity, talent, and new ideas, contributing to the intellectual vibrancy of the institution. For the city of London, international students contribute to the economy, enrich the cultural landscape, and enhance the city's global reputation.

"International students are a vital part of London's academic community," says Gore. "They bring new perspectives, challenge us to think differently, and contribute to the intellectual vibrancy of our institutions."

However, London's universities also face challenges. The high cost of tuition and living expenses can make it difficult for some students to afford a London education. The UK's withdrawal from the European Union has also created uncertainty for the higher education sector, particularly around research funding and student mobility.

Despite these challenges, London's universities remain committed to their mission of providing world-class education and research. They are adapting to the changing landscape of higher education, embracing new technologies, and expanding their global reach. London's universities are also playing a leading role in addressing global challenges, such as climate change, inequality, and social injustice.

"London's universities are a force for good in the world," says Thomson. "We are committed to using our knowledge and expertise to make a positive impact on society."

London's universities are not just institutions of learning; they are engines of innovation, catalysts for change, and beacons of hope. They are nurturing the next generation of global leaders, thinkers, and innovators who will shape the world of tomorrow. As London continues to evolve as a global city, its universities will remain a vital part of its identity, a testament to the city's enduring commitment to education, research, and the pursuit of knowledge.

CHAPTER 20: THE LONDON OLYMPICS 2012: SHOWCASING URBAN REGENERATION

The summer of 2012 was a defining moment for London. The city, adorned in Olympic regalia, buzzed with the energy of athletes, spectators, and volunteers from across the globe. The London Olympics was not merely a sporting event; it was a catalyst for urban regeneration, transforming a once-neglected area of East London into a thriving hub of activity and opportunity.

The Olympic Park, located in Stratford, was the epicentre of this transformation. Prior to the Games, the area was a post-industrial wasteland, scarred by decades of neglect. The Olympic bid, however, presented a unique opportunity to revitalize this area, not just for the two weeks of the Games, but for generations to come.

The construction of the Olympic Park was a feat of engineering and logistics, involving the creation of world-class sporting venues, parklands, and infrastructure. The iconic Olympic Stadium, with its distinctive swooping roofline, became a symbol of the Games, while the Aquatics Centre, with its graceful curves and undulating roof, was hailed as an architectural masterpiece.

But the Olympic Park was more than just a collection of impressive buildings. It was designed to be a sustainable and inclusive community, with new homes, schools, healthcare facilities, and cultural spaces. The parkland, with its waterways, meadows, and woodlands, became a haven for wildlife and a popular destination for recreation and relaxation.

"The London Olympics was a game-changer for East London," says Lord Sebastian Coe, Chairman of the London Organising Committee of the Olympic and Paralympic Games. "It transformed a neglected area into a vibrant and thriving community, creating new opportunities for local residents and attracting investment and businesses to the area."

The impact of the Olympics on London's development has been significant. The Games generated billions of pounds in economic activity, creating jobs, boosting tourism, and attracting investment. The Olympic Park has become a major cultural and sporting destination, hosting events like the London Marathon, the World Athletics Championships, and concerts by global superstars.

The regeneration of East London has also had a social impact. The new homes and facilities in the Olympic Park have provided much-needed affordable housing and improved the quality of life for local residents. The park itself has become a community hub, bringing people together from diverse backgrounds.

However, the legacy of the London Olympics is not without its critics. Some argue that the regeneration has not benefited all local residents equally, with some communities feeling displaced and marginalized. There are also concerns about the long-term sustainability of the Olympic Park, particularly given the high cost of maintaining the sporting venues.

"The Olympic legacy is a mixed bag," says Dr. Penny Bernstock, a researcher at the University of East London. "While there have been significant benefits, such as improved infrastructure and new housing, there are also concerns about gentrification and the lack of affordable housing."

Despite these challenges, the London Olympics has undoubtedly left a lasting legacy on the city. It has shown that major sporting events can be a catalyst for urban regeneration, transforming neglected areas into thriving communities. The Olympic Park stands as a testament to the power of vision, ambition, and collaboration, a reminder that even the most ambitious dreams can be realized.

As London continues to evolve, the Olympic Park will remain a symbol of the city's commitment to regeneration and renewal. It will continue to attract visitors, businesses, and residents, contributing to the city's economic and cultural vibrancy. The legacy of the London Olympics is a story that is still being written, a story of transformation, resilience, and the enduring power of the human spirit.

CHAPTER 21: LONDON'S START-UP ECOSYSTEM: BREEDING INNOVATION

In the heart of London, amidst the historic landmarks and bustling streets, a new wave of innovation is surging. It's a wave driven by a thriving start-up ecosystem, a dynamic network of entrepreneurs, investors, and support organizations that is transforming London into a global hub for innovation and entrepreneurship.

London's start-up scene is a vibrant tapestry, woven from threads of creativity, ambition, and technological prowess. From fintech disruptors to AI pioneers, from clean energy innovators to social entrepreneurs, London's start-ups are tackling some of the world's most pressing challenges and creating new opportunities for growth and prosperity.

"London is a magnet for entrepreneurial talent," says Eileen Burbidge, Partner at Passion Capital, a leading venture capital firm based in London. "The city's diversity, its access to global markets, and its supportive ecosystem make it an ideal place for start-ups to thrive."

The numbers speak for themselves. London is home to over 10,000 start-ups, employing over 250,000 people and generating billions in revenue. In 2022, London's tech sector attracted a record £24 billion in venture capital investment, surpassing New York and solidifying its position as a global leader in tech investment.

The success of London's start-up ecosystem is not accidental. It's the result of a confluence of factors, including a supportive government, a thriving venture capital scene, a diverse talent pool, and a culture that celebrates risk-taking and innovation.

The UK government has played a key role in fostering entrepreneurship. Initiatives such as the Seed Enterprise Investment Scheme (SEIS) and the Enterprise Investment Scheme (EIS) provide tax incentives for investors in early-stage companies, while Tech Nation, a network of tech entrepreneurs and experts, offers support and resources for start-ups.

London's venture capital scene is also thriving. The city is home to a large number of venture capital firms, including some of the most prestigious names in the industry. These firms provide crucial funding for start-ups, enabling them to scale and grow.

London's diverse talent pool is another key factor in its start-up success. The city attracts talented individuals from around the world, drawn by its vibrant culture, diverse economy, and global outlook. This diversity of talent fuels innovation and creativity, leading to new ideas and new ways of doing business.

London's start-up ecosystem is also characterized by a strong sense of community and collaboration. Co-working spaces, accelerator programs, and networking events provide opportunities for entrepreneurs to connect, share ideas, and learn from each other. This collaborative spirit is essential for the success of any start-up ecosystem.

However, London's start-up scene is not without its challenges. The high cost of living and operating a business in London can be a barrier for some start-ups. Brexit has also created uncertainty for the tech sector, particularly around immigration and access to European markets.

Despite these challenges, London's start-up ecosystem remains resilient and optimistic. The city's strengths, including its talent pool, diverse economy, and global connectivity, continue to make it an attractive destination for entrepreneurs. The government is also committed to supporting the sector, with initiatives like the Help to Grow scheme and the Future Fund: Breakthrough.

"London's start-up scene is a beacon of hope," says Burbidge. "It's a testament to the power of human ingenuity and the ability of people to come together to create something new. I believe that London's start-ups will continue to make a positive impact on the world."

London's start-up ecosystem is a story of ambition, innovation, and the power of collaboration. It's a story that's still being written, with new chapters unfolding every day. As London continues to evolve as a global city, its start-up scene is poised to play an increasingly important role in the city's future, driving economic growth, creating jobs, and solving global challenges.

CHAPTER 22:
THE SHARD AND LONDON'S EVOLVING SKYLINE

As the sun dips below the horizon, a kaleidoscope of colors paints the sky above London, illuminating a skyline that is both timeless and ever-changing. From the historic spires of Westminster Abbey to the gleaming glass facade of the Shard, London's skyline is a visual symphony of architectural styles, a testament to the city's rich history and dynamic present. The Shard, London's tallest building, is a symbol of this evolution, a towering monument to modern ambition and a testament to the city's embrace of architectural innovation.

The Shard, designed by renowned Italian architect Renzo Piano, is a marvel of engineering and design. Its 95 floors house offices, restaurants, a hotel, and residential apartments, creating a vertical village in the heart of the city. But the Shard is more than just a building; it's a symbol of London's aspirations, a statement of its confidence and ambition on the global stage.

"The Shard is a landmark building that has redefined London's skyline," says Peter Murray, Chairman of New London Architecture (NLA), an independent forum for discussion and debate about architecture and development in London. "It's a bold and innovative structure that has captured the imagination of people around the world."

The Shard's impact on London's skyline is undeniable. It dominates the view from many parts of the city, its sleek silhouette a striking contrast to the historic landmarks that surround it. The Shard has become a symbol of modern London, a city that embraces change and innovation while still respecting its heritage.

The Shard is just one example of the wave of modern architecture that is reshaping London's skyline. In recent years, the city has seen a proliferation of tall buildings, many of them designed by world-renowned architects. The Gherkin, the Walkie Talkie, and the Cheesegrater are just a few of the nicknames given to these new additions to the London skyline. This new wave of architecture is not without its critics. Some argue that these tall buildings are out of scale with their surroundings, that they damage London's historic character, and that they cater primarily to the wealthy elite. Others argue that they are a necessary part of London's growth and development, providing much-needed office space, housing, and amenities.

"The debate over tall buildings is a complex one," says Murray. "There are valid arguments on both sides. But I believe that tall buildings can enhance London's skyline if they are well-designed and thoughtfully integrated into their surroundings."

London's evolving skyline is a reflection of the city's dynamism and its ability to adapt to change. The city's architectural landscape is a constantly evolving canvas, shaped by economic, social, and cultural forces. The Shard and other modern buildings are a testament to London's ambition and its willingness to embrace new ideas.

London's skyline is also a reflection of the city's diversity. The buildings that make up the skyline are as diverse as the people who live and work in the city. They range from historic landmarks like St. Paul's Cathedral and the Houses of Parliament to modern icons like the Shard and the Gherkin.

This diversity is what makes London's skyline so unique and so fascinating.

"London's skyline is a visual representation of the city's history, its culture, and its people," says Murray. "It's a living, breathing organism that is constantly evolving and changing. It's a testament to London's enduring spirit and its ability to reinvent itself."

As London continues to grow and evolve, its skyline will undoubtedly continue to change. New buildings will rise, old buildings will be repurposed, and the city's architectural landscape will continue to evolve. The Shard and other modern buildings will remain a part of that landscape, symbols of London's ambition and its embrace of the future.

CHAPTER 23: LONDON'S ART SCENE: FROM TATE MODERN TO STREET ART

The pulse of London's artistic heart throbs not just in the hallowed halls of traditional galleries but also on its vibrant streets. The city's art scene, a dynamic fusion of established institutions and edgy urban creativity, has cemented London's position as a global art capital. From the iconic Tate Modern to the ever-evolving street art of Shoreditch, London's artistic landscape is a kaleidoscope of styles, movements, and expressions, reflecting the city's rich cultural diversity and unwavering spirit of innovation.

London's influence on global art trends is undeniable. The city has a long and illustrious history of artistic excellence, from the Renaissance masterpieces of Hans Holbein the Younger to the ground-breaking works of J.M.W. Turner and the Pre-Raphaelites. In the 20th century, London became a hub for modern and contemporary art, with movements like Pop Art and the Young British Artists emerging from the city's creative cauldron.

Today, London's art scene is more vibrant and diverse than ever before. The city boasts a wide range of art institutions, from world-renowned museums like the Tate Modern and the National Gallery to smaller, independent galleries showcasing emerging artists. London is also home to a thriving commercial art market, with auction houses like Sotheby's and Christie's regularly setting record prices for works of art.

"London's art scene is a microcosm of the global art world," says Iwona Blazwick, the former Director of the Whitechapel Gallery. "It's a place where artists from all over the world come to showcase their work, where collectors come to buy, and where art lovers come to be inspired."

The Tate Modern, housed in a former power station on the banks of the River Thames, is a symbol of London's contemporary art scene. Its vast Turbine Hall has hosted some of the most ambitious and thought-provoking installations of recent times, including Olafur Eliasson's "The Weather Project" and Ai Weiwei's "Sunflower Seeds." The Tate Modern's collection of modern and contemporary art is one of the most comprehensive in the world, featuring works by Picasso, Matisse, Warhol, and Hockney, among others.

But London's art scene is not confined to the Tate Modern or other traditional galleries. The city's streets have become a canvas for a new generation of artists, who use graffiti, murals, and other forms of street art to express their creativity and challenge the status quo. The East End, particularly Shoreditch and Brick Lane, is a hotbed of street art, with ever-changing murals adorning the walls and buildings.

"Street art has democratized the art world," says Ben Eine, a renowned street artist whose work has been exhibited in galleries around the world. "It's taken art out of the gallery and onto the streets, making it accessible to everyone."

London's street art is not just about aesthetics; it's also a form of social commentary and political activism. Street artists use their work to address issues such as climate change, social inequality, and political corruption. Banksy, perhaps the most famous street artist in the world, has used his work to challenge authority and provoke debate.

London's art scene is a reflection of the city's diversity and its openness to new ideas. The city's artists come from all walks of life, representing a wide range of cultures, backgrounds, and perspectives. This diversity is a source of strength, fuelling creativity and innovation.

"London's art scene is a melting pot of cultures and styles," says Blazwick. "It's a place where anything is possible, where the boundaries between high art and low art are blurred, and where new forms of artistic expression are constantly emerging."

The future of London's art scene is bright. The city's universities are producing a new generation of talented artists, and new galleries and art spaces are opening all the time. London's position as a global financial centre also ensures a steady flow of investment in the art market.

London's art scene is a vibrant and dynamic ecosystem, a testament to the city's rich cultural heritage and its enduring spirit of creativity. From the hallowed halls of the Tate Modern to the vibrant streets of Shoreditch, London is a city where art is celebrated, debated, and embraced. The city's influence on global art trends is undeniable, and its artistic legacy will continue to inspire and challenge for generations to come.

CHAPTER 24: THE LONDON PLAN: STRATEGIC URBAN DEVELOPMENT FOR THE 21ST CENTURY

London is a city in constant flux, a dynamic metropolis where the old and new collide. As the city grows and evolves, so too must its approach to urban planning. The London Plan, a strategic document that sets out the vision for the city's development over the next two decades, is a testament to London's commitment to sustainable and inclusive growth. This ambitious plan addresses the complex challenges facing the city, from housing affordability and climate change to transport infrastructure and economic development. It's a roadmap for a future London that is greener, fairer, and more resilient.

The London Plan is not just a technical document; it's a vision for a city that works for everyone. It prioritizes affordable housing, sustainable transport, and the creation of vibrant and inclusive communities. The plan also recognizes the importance of green spaces, cultural heritage, and the need to protect London's unique character.

"The London Plan is a bold and ambitious vision for the future of our city," says Jules Pipe, Deputy Mayor for Planning,

Regeneration and Skills. "It sets out a clear path for how we can create a London that is fairer, greener, and more prosperous for all."

The plan is based on extensive research and consultation with Londoners from all walks of life. It takes into account the city's diverse needs and aspirations, from the young professional seeking affordable housing to the elderly resident in need of accessible transport. The plan also considers the impact of global trends, such as climate change and technological innovation, on London's future.

"The London Plan is not just about bricks and mortar," says Pipe. "It's about creating a city that is sustainable, resilient, and inclusive. It's about ensuring that London remains a great place to live, work, and visit for generations to come."

The plan sets out a number of ambitious targets, including the delivery of 50,000 new affordable homes each year, a significant increase in the use of public transport, and a reduction in carbon emissions to net-zero by 2030. The plan also calls for the creation of new green spaces, the protection of historic buildings, and the promotion of a circular economy. These targets are not without their challenges. London's housing crisis is a complex issue, driven by factors such as population growth, limited land availability, and rising construction costs. The city's transport system is already under strain, and increasing the use of public transport will require significant investment in new infrastructure.

The London Plan is also a source of debate and controversy. Some critics argue that the plan's focus on high-density development will lead to the loss of green spaces and the destruction of historic buildings. Others argue that the plan does not go far enough in addressing the needs of London's most vulnerable communities.

"The London Plan is a compromise," says Dr. Nicola Livingstone, a researcher at the Centre for London think tank. "It tries to balance the need for growth with the need to protect the environment and ensure social equity. It's not perfect, but it's a step in the right direction."

Despite these challenges and criticisms, the London Plan remains a landmark document. It's a testament to the city's commitment to sustainable and inclusive growth, and it sets a high bar for other cities around the world. The plan's success will depend on the collaboration and commitment of a wide range of stakeholders, from government agencies and developers to community groups and businesses.

The London Plan is a living document, subject to review and revision as the city's needs and priorities evolve. However, its core principles of sustainability, inclusivity, and resilience are likely to remain at the heart of London's urban development for many years to come.

The London Plan is a roadmap for the future, a blueprint for a city that is not only a global powerhouse but also a liveable, sustainable, and equitable home for all its residents. It's a vision that is both ambitious and achievable, a testament to the enduring spirit of London and its ability to reinvent itself for the 21st century.

CHAPTER 25: LONDON'S LEGAL HUB: THE ROYAL COURTS OF JUSTICE AND INTERNATIONAL LAW

Beneath the imposing Gothic spires of the Royal Courts of Justice (RCJ), a complex legal ecosystem thrives, reinforcing London's status as a global centre for law and justice. The RCJ, a majestic Victorian edifice situated in the heart of London, is more than just a court building; it's a symbol of the city's legal heritage, a testament to its commitment to the rule of law, and a hub for international legal activity.

The RCJ, often simply referred to as the Law Courts, is the headquarters of the Senior Courts of England and Wales, the highest courts in the land. Within its grand halls and ornate courtrooms, some of the most important legal cases in the country are heard. These cases often have far-reaching implications, not just for the UK, but for the wider world. The RCJ's judgments are frequently cited in other jurisdictions, influencing the development of legal principles and shaping the course of international law.

"The Royal Courts of Justice are a cornerstone of the UK legal system," says Lord Burnett of Maldon, the Lord Chief Justice of England and Wales. "They are a symbol of our commitment to justice, fairness, and the rule of law."

The RCJ's significance extends beyond its role as a court building. It's also a hub for the legal profession, attracting lawyers, barristers, and legal scholars from around the world. The Inns of Court, a collection of historic legal societies located nearby, play a key role in training and regulating the legal profession in England and Wales. The Inns of Court also offer a rich cultural and social life for the legal community, with lectures, dinners, and other events taking place throughout the year.

"London is a global legal centre," says Lord Burnett. "It's home to some of the world's leading law firms, barristers' chambers, and legal institutions. The city's legal expertise is sought after by clients from around the world."

London's legal sector is a significant contributor to the UK economy, generating billions of pounds in revenue each year. The city's law firms advise on complex cross-border transactions, resolve high-stakes commercial disputes, and represent clients in international arbitrations. London is also home to a number of international legal institutions, such as the International Maritime Organization and the Commonwealth Secretariat, which play a crucial role in shaping global law and policy.

London's legal hub status is not just about its economic contribution. It's also about the city's commitment to justice, fairness, and the rule of law. London's courts are known for their independence, impartiality, and adherence to due process. The city's legal profession is also committed to pro bono work, providing free legal services to those who cannot afford them.

"London is a city that values justice and fairness," says Lady Hale of Richmond, former President of the Supreme Court of the United Kingdom. "It's a place where people from all walks of life can access justice, regardless of their background or circumstances."

London's legal hub status is not without its challenges. The UK's withdrawal from the European Union has created uncertainty for the legal sector, particularly around the recognition of UK court judgments and the ability of UK lawyers to practice in EU member states. The high cost of legal services in London can also be a barrier to access to justice for some individuals and businesses.

Despite these challenges, London remains a global legal powerhouse. The city's deep legal expertise, its robust legal infrastructure, and its commitment to the rule of law continue to attract clients and businesses from around the world. London's legal sector is also adapting to the changing landscape of international law, embracing new technologies and expanding its reach into emerging markets.

"London's legal hub status is not a given," says Lord Burnett. "It's something that we need to work hard to maintain and strengthen. But I'm confident that London will continue to be a leading centre for law and justice in the 21st century."

London's legal hub is a microcosm of the global legal system, a place where the world's legal challenges are met and resolved. It's a place of tradition, innovation, and the pursuit of justice. As the world becomes more interconnected and complex, London's legal hub will continue to play a vital role in shaping the future of international law and ensuring that justice is accessible to all.

CHAPTER 26: THE LONDON MARATHON: A GLOBAL SPORTING PHENOMENON

The rhythmic pounding of thousands of feet, the roar of the crowds, and the iconic landmarks flashing by—this is the London Marathon, a global sporting phenomenon that encapsulates the city's spirit of endurance, community, and spectacle. Held annually since 1981, the marathon has grown from a local race to an internationally renowned event, attracting elite athletes and amateur runners alike. The marathon's success is a testament to London's ability to host major international sporting events, showcasing the city's logistical capabilities, cultural vibrancy, and global appeal.

The London Marathon's route is a 26.2-mile odyssey through the heart of London, winding past iconic landmarks like the Cutty Sark, Tower Bridge, and Buckingham Palace. The race starts in Greenwich, home to the Royal Observatory and the Prime Meridian of the World, and finishes on The Mall, the grand avenue leading to Buckingham Palace. Along the way, runners are cheered on by hundreds of thousands of spectators, creating an electric atmosphere that is unique to the London Marathon.

"The London Marathon is more than just a race," says Hugh Brasher, Event Director of the London Marathon. "It's a celebration of human endeavour, a showcase of London's diversity, and a platform for charitable giving. It's an event that brings people together from all walks of life."

The marathon's impact on London is significant. It generates over £100 million for the UK economy each year, through tourism, hospitality, and retail spending. The event also raises millions of pounds for charity, with runners often raising funds for causes close to their hearts. In 2022, the London Marathon raised a record-breaking £70 million for charity, making it the largest single-day fundraising event in the world.

"The London Marathon is a force for good," says Brasher. "It inspires people to challenge themselves, to push their limits, and to give back to their communities."

The marathon's success is due in part to London's unique blend of history, culture, and infrastructure. The city's iconic landmarks provide a stunning backdrop for the race, while its well-connected transport network makes it easy for spectators to access the route. London's diverse population also contributes to the marathon's vibrancy, with runners and spectators from all over the world coming together to celebrate the event.

"London is the perfect city for a marathon," says Paula Radcliffe, three-time winner of the London Marathon and former world record holder. "It's a city with a rich history, a vibrant culture, and a passion for sport. The support from the crowds is incredible, and it really pushes you to your limits."

The London Marathon's success has also paved the way for other major sporting events to be held in London. The city has hosted the Olympic Games twice, in 1908 and 2012, and is set to host the UEFA European Championship in 2024.London is also a regular host of major sporting events like the Wimbledon Championships, the World Athletics Championships, and the NFL London Games.

"London has a proven track record of hosting major international sporting events," says Sadiq Khan, Mayor of London. "The city's infrastructure, its expertise, and its passion for sport make it an ideal host for global events."

The London Marathon is a testament to London's ability to organize and deliver world-class sporting events. It's a showcase of the city's logistical capabilities, its cultural vibrancy, and its global appeal. The marathon's legacy extends far beyond the event itself, inspiring people to get active, raise money for charity, and celebrate the power of human spirit.

The London Marathon is a global sporting phenomenon that continues to capture the imagination of the world. It's a symbol of London's enduring spirit, its passion for sport, and its ability to bring people together. As the marathon continues to evolve, it will undoubtedly remain a highlight of the sporting calendar, a testament to the city's ability to stage world-class events, and a source of pride for Londoners for many years to come.

CHAPTER 27: CANARY WHARF: THE RISE OF A NEW FINANCIAL DISTRICT

The gleaming towers of Canary Wharf pierce the London skyline, a testament to the city's ambition, resilience, and unwavering drive for economic growth. Once a desolate dockland, Canary Wharf has transformed into a thriving financial district, a symbol of London's ability to reinvent itself and adapt to the changing tides of global finance. This modern business hub, with its sleek skyscrapers, bustling waterfront, and vibrant community, is a microcosm of London's dynamism and its unwavering commitment to progress.

The story of Canary Wharf is a remarkable tale of urban regeneration. In the 1980s, the Docklands, once the heart of London's maritime trade, had fallen into decline. The closure of the docks left behind a landscape of derelict warehouses and abandoned wharves. However, a group of visionary developers saw the potential of this forgotten corner of London. Led by Canadian businessman Paul Reichmann, they embarked on an ambitious project to transform the Docklands into a new financial district.

"Canary Wharf was a bold and ambitious project," says Sir George Iacobescu, former Chairman and Chief Executive Officer of Canary Wharf Group. "It was a gamble, but we believed in the potential of this area and its ability to become a world-class business destination."

The development of Canary Wharf was a massive undertaking, involving the construction of millions of square feet of office space, residential towers, shopping malls, and transport infrastructure. The centrepiece of the development was One Canada Square, a 50-story skyscraper that became the tallest building in the UK upon its completion in 1991.

The rise of Canary Wharf was not without its challenges. The early years were marked by financial difficulties and scepticism from the established financial community in the City of London. However, the development persevered, attracting major banks and financial institutions, including HSBC, Citigroup, and Barclays.

Today, Canary Wharf is a thriving business district, home to over 120,000 workers and a major contributor to the UK economy. Its gleaming towers house a diverse range of businesses, from financial services and technology to media and professional services. The area is also a popular destination for shopping, dining, and entertainment, with a variety of shops, restaurants, bars, and cultural venues.

"Canary Wharf is a vibrant and dynamic community," says Shobi Khan, CEO of Canary Wharf Group. "It's a place where people come to work, live, and play. It's a testament to the vision and determination of those who believed in the potential of this area."

The impact of Canary Wharf on London's economy and urban landscape has been significant. It has created thousands of jobs, attracted billions of pounds in investment, and revitalized a once-neglected area of the city. Canary Wharf has also played a role in shifting London's centre of gravity eastward, contributing to the regeneration of the Docklands and surrounding areas.

"Canary Wharf has been a catalyst for growth and regeneration in East London," says Khan. "It has transformed the area into a vibrant and thriving hub of activity, creating new opportunities for local residents and businesses."

However, Canary Wharf has also been criticized for its lack of affordability and its isolation from the rest of London. The high cost of living and working in Canary Wharf has led to concerns about social exclusion and inequality. The area's reliance on public transport, particularly the Docklands Light Railway (DLR) and the Jubilee line, has also raised concerns about its vulnerability to disruptions.

Despite these challenges, Canary Wharf remains a symbol of London's ambition and its ability to reinvent itself. The development continues to evolve, with new projects underway to expand its office space, residential offerings, and cultural amenities. Canary Wharf is also embracing new technologies, such as smart city initiatives and sustainable building practices, to create a more liveable and resilient community.

"Canary Wharf is a testament to the power of human ingenuity and the ability to create something extraordinary from nothing," says Khan. "It's a symbol of London's resilience, its ambition, and its unwavering commitment to progress."

The story of Canary Wharf is a reminder that even the most ambitious dreams can be realized with vision, determination, and collaboration. It's a story of urban regeneration, economic growth, and the creation of a new community. As London continues to evolve, Canary Wharf will remain a vital part of its identity, a symbol of its ambition and its unwavering drive for success.

CHAPTER 28: LONDON'S CHINATOWN: A MICROCOSM OF CULTURAL INTEGRATION

In the heart of London's vibrant West End, a riot of color, sound, and aroma beckons visitors into a world apart. This is Chinatown, a bustling enclave that embodies the city's rich multicultural tapestry. Beyond its ornate pagoda-style gates and lantern-strewn streets, Chinatown serves as a microcosm of London's cultural integration, a testament to the city's ability to embrace diversity, foster cultural exchange, and create spaces where different communities can thrive.

Chinatown's history is intertwined with London's evolving identity as a global city. Chinese immigrants first arrived in London in the 18th century, establishing a community in the Limehouse area of the East End. However, it wasn't until the mid-20th century, with the influx of immigrants from Hong Kong, that Chinatown as we know it today began to take shape. Gerrard Street, the epicentre of Chinatown, is a vibrant thoroughfare lined with Chinese restaurants, bakeries, supermarkets, and shops. The air is thick with the scent of spices and roasting meats, while the sounds of Cantonese, Mandarin, and English mingle in a lively cacophony. The street is a popular destination for both tourists and locals, drawn by its authentic cuisine, vibrant atmosphere, and cultural offerings.

"Chinatown is a dynamic and ever-evolving community," says Dr. Peng Wang, a sociologist who has studied the area extensively. "It's a place where Chinese culture is preserved and celebrated, but also a place where it interacts and adapts to the wider London context."

Chinatown's cultural significance extends beyond its culinary and commercial offerings. The London Chinatown Chinese Association (LCCA), a community organization founded in 1979, plays a crucial role in promoting Chinese culture and heritage. The LCCA organizes events such as the Chinese New Year celebrations, which draw thousands of visitors each year, and provides support services for the local community.

"Chinatown is a symbol of Chinese identity and heritage in London," says Edmund Yeo, Chairman of the LCCA. "It's a place where we can connect with our roots, share our culture with others, and contribute to the wider London community."

Chinatown's success as a cultural hub is a testament to London's tolerant and inclusive ethos. Unlike Chinatowns in some other cities, which have become isolated enclaves, London's Chinatown is fully integrated into the city's fabric. Its residents and businesses interact with the wider community, contributing to the city's economic and cultural vibrancy.

"London's Chinatown is a model of cultural integration," says Dr. Wang. "It's a place where different cultures coexist and enrich each other. It's a testament to the city's openness and diversity."

However, Chinatown also faces challenges. The rising cost of rent and gentrification are putting pressure on small businesses and long-time residents. There are also concerns about the impact of tourism on the area's authenticity and cultural integrity.

"Chinatown needs to strike a balance between preserving its cultural heritage and adapting to the changing needs of the community," says Yeo. "We need to find ways to support small businesses, preserve affordable housing, and ensure that Chinatown remains a vibrant and welcoming place for everyone."

The future of Chinatown is uncertain, but its resilience and adaptability give cause for optimism. The community is actively engaged in shaping its own destiny, working with local authorities and businesses to address the challenges facing the area. Chinatown is also embracing new technologies and trends, such as online shopping and social media, to reach a wider audience and promote its cultural offerings.

"Chinatown is a survivor," says Dr. Wang. "It has weathered many storms over the years, from economic downturns to social unrest. But it has always managed to adapt and thrive. I believe that Chinatown will continue to be a vibrant and important part of London's cultural landscape for many years to come."

London's Chinatown is a microcosm of the city's multicultural character, a testament to its ability to embrace diversity and create spaces where different cultures can flourish. It's a place where tradition and modernity coexist, where the past meets the present, and where the future is being shaped. Chinatown is a reminder that London is a global city, a melting pot of cultures, and a place where anything is possible.

CHAPTER 29: THE LONDON EYE: REDEFINING THE CITY'S SKYLINE AND TOURISM

In the heart of London, a colossal Ferris wheel rises above the River Thames, its graceful arc dominating the skyline. The London Eye, a modern marvel of engineering and design, has become a beloved symbol of the city, a testament to its spirit of innovation and its commitment to tourism.

The Eye's inception was a bold vision born at the turn of the millennium. Originally intended as a temporary structure to mark the new millennium, the London Eye quickly captured the hearts of Londoners and tourists alike. Its popularity led to its permanent installation, and it has since become one of the most visited paid tourist attractions in the UK.

"The London Eye is more than just a Ferris wheel," says Sunny Jouhal, General Manager of the London Eye. "It's a symbol of modern London, a feat of engineering, and a unique way to experience the city's iconic landmarks."

The Eye's impact on London's skyline is undeniable. Standing at 135 meters (443 feet) tall, it's the tallest cantilevered observation wheel in the world. Its 32 capsules, each holding up to 25 passengers, offer unparalleled panoramic views of the city, stretching up to 40 kilometres (25 miles) on a clear day. The Eye has become an iconic landmark, its silhouette instantly recognizable and often featured in films, television shows, and photographs.

"The London Eye has redefined the city's skyline," says Jouhal. "It's a modern icon that complements the city's historic landmarks, creating a unique blend of old and new."

The Eye's impact on London's economy has also been significant. It attracts over 3.5 million visitors each year, generating millions of pounds in revenue for the city. The Eye's success has also spurred the development of other attractions along the South Bank, such as the SEA LIFE London Aquarium and the London Dungeon, creating a vibrant cultural and entertainment hub.

"The London Eye has been a catalyst for the regeneration of the South Bank," says Kate Nicholls, Chief Executive of UK-Hospitality, the trade association for the hospitality industry. "It has attracted investment, created jobs, and boosted tourism in the area."

The Eye's popularity has also had a ripple effect on the wider economy. It has boosted demand for hotels, restaurants, and other tourist services, contributing to the growth of London's tourism industry. The Eye has also become a popular venue for corporate events and private parties, generating additional revenue for the city.

"The London Eye is a major contributor to London's economy," says Nicholls. "It's a magnet for tourists, and it generates significant revenue for the city's hospitality and tourism sectors."

However, the Eye's success has not been without controversy. Some critics argue that it is an eyesore, a blot on the landscape that detracts from the city's historic beauty. Others raise concerns about its environmental impact, particularly its energy consumption and carbon footprint.

"The London Eye is a symbol of unsustainable tourism," says Justin Francis, CEO of Responsible Travel, a travel company that promotes sustainable tourism practices. "It's a high-energy-consuming attraction that generates significant carbon emissions. We need to find more sustainable ways to promote tourism in London."

Despite these criticisms, the London Eye remains a popular and beloved attraction. Its unique design, stunning views, and iconic status have made it a must-visit destination for tourists and locals alike. The Eye's operators are also committed to sustainability, implementing measures to reduce its environmental impact.

"The London Eye is a sustainable attraction," says Jouhal. "We're constantly looking for ways to reduce our energy consumption and carbon footprint. We're also committed to supporting local businesses and promoting sustainable tourism practices."

The London Eye is a testament to the city's ability to embrace innovation and create world-class attractions. Its impact on London's skyline, economy, and tourism industry is undeniable. As London continues to evolve as a global city, the London Eye will remain a symbol of its modernity, its creativity, and its commitment to providing a memorable experience for visitors from around the world.

CHAPTER 30: LONDON'S TECH START-UPS: DRIVING GLOBAL INNOVATION

In the heart of London, amidst the city's iconic landmarks and historic streets, a technological revolution is brewing. A vibrant ecosystem of tech start-ups has emerged, fuelled by a confluence of factors that make London a global hub for innovation and entrepreneurship. From fintech disruptors challenging traditional banking models to AI pioneers pushing the boundaries of machine learning, London's tech start-ups are shaping the future of industries and redefining the way we live and work.

London's tech scene is a diverse and dynamic landscape, encompassing a wide range of sectors, including fintech, healthtech, edtech, cleantech, and more. The city's start-ups are not just innovating in technology; they are also disrupting traditional business models, creating new markets, and solving complex global challenges.

"London is a hotbed of tech talent and innovation," says Gerard Grech, Founding CEO of Tech Nation, a UK network supporting tech entrepreneurs. "The city's unique blend of creativity, diversity, and global outlook makes it an ideal environment for start-ups to thrive."

The numbers paint a compelling picture. London is home to

over 10,000 tech start-ups, employing over 300,000 people and contributing billions of pounds to the UK economy each year. In 2022 alone, London's tech sector attracted over £24 billion in venture capital investment, surpassing New York and solidifying its position as the leading tech hub in Europe.

This remarkable growth is not a coincidence. London's tech ecosystem is supported by a robust infrastructure that includes world-class universities, research institutions, and a thriving network of accelerators, incubators, and co-working spaces. The city also benefits from a supportive government that has implemented policies to encourage innovation and entrepreneurship, such as tax incentives for investors and streamlined visa processes for tech talent.

London's tech start-ups are not just innovating for the sake of innovation. They are driven by a desire to make a positive impact on the world. For example, companies like BenevolentAI are using artificial intelligence to develop new drugs and treatments for diseases, while others like Octopus Energy are disrupting the energy sector with innovative clean energy solutions.

"London's tech start-ups are not just building businesses; they are building a better future," says Grech. "They are tackling some of the world's most pressing challenges, from climate change to healthcare, and they are doing it with passion, creativity, and a relentless drive for innovation."

The success of London's tech start-ups is also a testament to the city's diverse talent pool. London attracts entrepreneurs and innovators from around the world, drawn by its vibrant culture, diverse economy, and global outlook. This diversity of talent fuels innovation and creativity, leading to new ideas and new ways of doing business.

"London's diversity is one of its greatest strengths," says Poppy Gustafsson, CEO of Darktrace, a leading cybersecurity company based in London. "It's a place where people from all walks of life can come together and create something extraordinary."

However, London's tech scene is not without its challenges. The high cost of living and operating a business in London can be a barrier for some start-ups. The UK's withdrawal from the European Union has also created uncertainty for the tech sector, particularly around immigration and access to European markets.

Despite these challenges, London's tech scene remains resilient and optimistic. The city's strengths, including its talent pool, diverse economy, and global connectivity, continue to make it an attractive destination for tech entrepreneurs. The government is also committed to supporting the sector, with initiatives like the Help to Grow: Digital scheme and the Tech Nation visa route.

"London's tech scene is a beacon of hope for the future," says Grech. "It's a testament to the power of human ingenuity and the ability of people to come together to create something new. I believe that London's tech start-ups will continue to lead the way in global innovation and make a positive impact on the world."

London's tech start-ups are a driving force behind the city's economic growth and global influence. They are creating jobs, attracting investment, and shaping the future of industries. As London continues to evolve as a global tech hub, its start-ups will play an increasingly important role in driving innovation and creating a better future for all.

CHAPTER 31: THE CHANGING FACE OF THE EAST END: URBAN REGENERATION IN ACTION

Venture eastwards from the gleaming towers of the City, past the historic Tower of London, and you'll find yourself in a district that has undergone a remarkable transformation. The East End, once synonymous with poverty, crime, and industrial decline, is now a vibrant hub of creativity, entrepreneurship, and cultural diversity. This ongoing metamorphosis, driven by a combination of public and private investment, has far-reaching implications not only for London but also for urban regeneration efforts worldwide.

The East End's history is a complex tapestry woven from threads of immigration, industry, and social change. It was once a melting pot of cultures, a place where waves of immigrants, from Huguenots to Bangladeshis, made their home and contributed to the city's rich tapestry. The area was also a centre of industry, with bustling docks, factories, and workshops lining the River Thames.

However, the decline of manufacturing and the closure of the docks in the 20th century plunged the East End into economic hardship. The area became synonymous with poverty, deprivation, and social unrest. But amidst the challenges, a spirit of resilience and creativity endured, and the seeds of regeneration were sown.

The first wave of regeneration came in the form of the Docklands redevelopment in the 1980s. This ambitious project transformed abandoned docklands into a gleaming financial district, Canary Wharf, attracting investment, businesses, and new residents to the area. However, the benefits of this regeneration were not evenly distributed, and many long-time residents felt displaced and marginalized.

The second wave of regeneration, which began in the 2000s, has taken a more holistic approach, focusing on community-led initiatives and sustainable development. This wave has been driven by a combination of factors, including public investment in infrastructure and housing, the rise of the creative industries, and the influx of young professionals and artists drawn to the area's affordability and vibrant atmosphere.

"The East End is a fascinating case study in urban regeneration," says Dr. Penny Bernstock, an urban geographer at Queen Mary University of London. "It's a place where we can see the challenges and opportunities of urban change, the tensions between gentrification and community development, and the potential for creating a more equitable and sustainable city."

The transformation of the East End is evident in its changing landscape. Former industrial sites have been repurposed as creative hubs, such as the Old Truman Brewery in Brick Lane, which now houses studios, galleries, and shops. The once-neglected canals have been revitalized, becoming popular destinations for walking, cycling, and boating. New residential developments, such as the Olympic Village, have brought a mix of housing options to the area, attracting a diverse range of residents.

"The East End is a constantly evolving landscape," says Paul Brickell, Executive Director of Regeneration and Community Partnerships at the London Legacy Development Corporation. "It's a place where new ideas and initiatives are constantly being tested and implemented. It's a laboratory for urban regeneration."

The East End's regeneration has had a profound impact on London as a whole. It has expanded the city's cultural and creative offerings, attracted new investment and businesses, and provided much-needed affordable housing. The area's diversity and vibrancy have also made it a popular destination for tourists and locals alike.

However, the regeneration of the East End has not been without its controversies. The rapid pace of change has led to concerns about gentrification and displacement, with long-time residents feeling priced out of the area. There are also concerns about the loss of the East End's unique character and cultural identity.

"The East End is at a crossroads," says Bernstock. "The challenge is to find a way to balance the needs of new residents and businesses with the preservation of the area's heritage and community spirit."

The future of the East End is uncertain, but its potential is undeniable. The area's ongoing transformation is a testament to the power of urban regeneration to create more liveable, inclusive, and sustainable communities. The lessons learned from the East End's experience can inform urban development efforts in other cities around the world, demonstrating that even the most challenging areas can be revitalized and transformed.

CHAPTER 32: LONDON'S MUSLIM COMMUNITY: INTEGRATION AND INFLUENCE

The melodic call to prayer echoing through the streets of Whitechapel, the vibrant bustle of Eid celebrations in Trafalgar Square, and the intellectual discussions in the East London Mosque—these are just glimpses into the dynamic and diverse world of London's Muslim community. With over 1.3 million Muslims residing in the city, Islam is the second largest religion in London, representing approximately 15% of the population. This growing community is not only a significant demographic presence but also a vital contributor to London's cultural, social, and economic fabric.

London's Muslim community is a microcosm of the global Muslim diaspora, reflecting a rich tapestry of cultures, nationalities, and traditions. From Pakistani and Bangladeshi communities with roots dating back to the post-war era to newer arrivals from Somalia, Afghanistan, and the Middle East, London's Muslims represent a diverse array of backgrounds and perspectives.

"London's Muslim community is a testament to the city's multiculturalism," says Shelina Jan Mohamed, author of *Love in a Headscarf* and a prominent voice on British Muslim identity. "It's a place where people from all over the world come together, united by their faith but also enriched by their unique cultural heritage."

The impact of London's Muslim community is felt across various spheres of city life. Economically, Muslims contribute significantly to the city's workforce, with entrepreneurs and professionals working across various sectors, from finance and technology to healthcare and education. They have also established a thriving network of businesses, from halal restaurants and grocery stores to Islamic fashion boutiques and travel agencies.

"London's Muslim community is an integral part of the city's economy," says Dr. Abdul Bari, Chairman of the East London Mosque. "We contribute to the city's prosperity through our businesses, our skills, and our hard work."

Culturally, London's Muslim community enriches the city's cultural landscape with its unique traditions, festivals, and artistic expressions. Events like Eid al-Fitr and Eid al-Adha are celebrated with great fanfare, attracting Londoners from all backgrounds. Islamic art and calligraphy are increasingly showcased in galleries and museums, while Muslim musicians and filmmakers are gaining recognition for their creative contributions.

"London's Muslim community is a source of cultural richness and diversity," says Janmohamed. "We bring new perspectives, new ideas, and new forms of artistic expression to the city's cultural scene."

London's Muslim community is also actively engaged in civic and political life. Muslim MPs, councillors, and community leaders play a vital role in representing the interests of their constituents and advocating for policies that benefit the wider community. The community is also involved in various charitable and volunteer initiatives, contributing to the social fabric of the city.

"London's Muslim community is a force for good in the city," says Bari. "We are committed to building strong and inclusive communities, promoting social cohesion, and making a positive contribution to society."

However, London's Muslim community also faces challenges. Islamophobia and discrimination remain significant concerns, with hate crimes and negative media portrayals impacting the lives of many Muslims. The community also grapples with issues of integration, identity, and the balance between faith and modernity.

"The challenges facing London's Muslim community are real," says Janmohamed. "But we are resilient, and we are determined to build a better future for ourselves and our children. We believe that London is a city of opportunity, a place where we can thrive and make a positive contribution to society."

The future of London's Muslim community is intertwined with the future of London itself. As the city continues to evolve and diversify, so too will its Muslim community. The challenges are significant, but the opportunities are even greater. With its rich heritage, vibrant culture, and commitment to social justice, London's Muslim community is poised to play an increasingly important role in shaping the city's future.

CHAPTER 33: THE O2 ARENA: LONDON AS AN ENTERTAINMENT POWERHOUSE

The energy is palpable as a sold-out crowd of 20,000 fans roars with excitement. Lights flash, music pulsates, and a global superstar takes the stage. This electrifying scene, unfolding beneath the iconic white dome of the O2 Arena, encapsulates London's status as a global entertainment powerhouse. The O2, a versatile venue hosting everything from concerts and sporting events to exhibitions and conferences, is a testament to the city's ability to attract top talent, host world-class events, and cater to a diverse range of audiences.

The O2's story is one of transformation and ambition. Originally built as the Millennium Dome to celebrate the turn of the millennium, the structure faced criticism for its high cost and lack of purpose. However, a decade later, it was reborn as the O2 Arena, a state-of-the-art entertainment venue that has since become one of the busiest arenas in the world.

"The O2 is a symbol of London's resilience and creativity," says Steve Sayer, VP & General Manager of The O2. "It's a testament to the city's ability to reinvent itself and adapt to changing times."

The O2's impact on London's entertainment scene is undeniable. It has hosted some of the biggest names in music, including Beyoncé, Prince, and The Rolling Stones. It has also been the stage for major sporting events, such as the ATP Finals tennis tournament and the NBA London Game. The O2's diverse program of events attracts millions of visitors each year, contributing significantly to the city's economy and cultural vibrancy.

"The O2 is a magnet for world-class entertainment," says Sayer. "It's a place where people come to experience the best that the world has to offer."

The O2's success is due in part to its unique location and design. Situated on the Greenwich Peninsula, a revitalized area of East London, the O2 is easily accessible by public transport and offers stunning views of the city skyline. Its distinctive dome, the largest single-span roof structure in the world, has become an iconic landmark. The O2's flexible design allows it to host a wide range of events, from intimate concerts to large-scale sporting events.

"The O2 is a world-class venue," says Sayer. "Its unique design and flexible space make it ideal for hosting a wide range of events. It's a testament to the ingenuity and creativity of its designers and builders."

The O2's impact extends beyond the entertainment industry. It has become a catalyst for regeneration in the Greenwich Peninsula, attracting new businesses, residents, and visitors to the area. The O2's success has also boosted London's reputation as a global entertainment hub, attracting more events and investment to the city.

"The O2 has been a game-changer for the Greenwich Peninsula," says Sayer. "It has transformed the area into a thriving entertainment district, creating jobs and opportunities for local residents."

The O2's success has not been without its challenges. The COVID-19 pandemic hit the entertainment industry hard, forcing the O2 to close its doors for several months. However, the arena has since reopened, and its diverse program of events is helping to revive London's entertainment scene.

"The O2 is resilient," says Sayer. "It has weathered the storm of the pandemic and emerged stronger than ever. We're committed to providing a safe and enjoyable experience for our visitors, and we're excited about the future of the O2."

The O2 Arena is a testament to London's status as a global entertainment powerhouse. It's a symbol of the city's creativity, diversity, and ambition. It's a place where people come together to celebrate the best of music, sport, and culture. The O2's success is a reminder that London is a city that never stands still, a city that is constantly evolving and reinventing itself. As the world emerges from the pandemic, the O2 is poised to play a key role in the revival of the entertainment industry, bringing joy, excitement, and inspiration to millions of people.

CHAPTER 34: LONDON'S LUXURY REAL ESTATE: A GLOBAL INVESTMENT HAVEN

The gleaming facades of luxury apartments rise against the historic backdrop of London's skyline, reflecting a global interest in the city's prime real estate. From opulent penthouses overlooking Hyde Park to sprawling mansions nestled in leafy enclaves, London's luxury property market has become a magnet for international investors, drawn by the city's stability, prestige, and potential for high returns. This influx of global capital has transformed London's property landscape, creating a complex and dynamic market with far-reaching economic, social, and cultural implications.

London's luxury real estate market is a global phenomenon, attracting buyers from all corners of the world. In recent years, investors from Russia, China, the Middle East, and beyond have flocked to London, seeking to park their wealth in safe and stable assets. The city's strong legal system, transparent property market, and reputation as a global financial centre make it an attractive destination for high-net-worth individuals and institutional investors.

"London is a global safe haven for real estate investment,"

says Liam Bailey, global head of research at Knight Frank, a leading real estate consultancy. "It's a city with a stable political system, a strong legal framework, and a track record of delivering solid returns on investment. These factors make London an attractive destination for investors seeking to diversify their portfolios and protect their wealth."

The impact of international investment on London's property market has been profound. It has driven up prices, fuelled demand for luxury developments, and transformed the city's skyline. In prime central London, the average price of a luxury property now exceeds £10 million, making it one of the most expensive property markets in the world.

However, the influx of international investment has not been without controversy. The rise in property prices has exacerbated London's housing affordability crisis, making it increasingly difficult for locals to buy or rent homes. The proliferation of luxury developments has also raised concerns about gentrification and the loss of community character.

"The impact of international investment on London's property market is a double-edged sword," says Rory Stewart, former Member of Parliament for Penrith and The Border and former Secretary of State for International Development. "On the one hand, it has brought much-needed investment and created jobs. On the other hand, it has pushed up prices and made housing unaffordable for many Londoners."

The London property market is a complex ecosystem, shaped by a multitude of factors, including economic conditions, government policies, and global trends. The influx of international investment is just one piece of this puzzle, but it's a significant one. The challenge for London is to find a way to balance the benefits of international investment with the need to create a more affordable and equitable housing market. The government has taken steps to address these concerns, introducing measures such as an additional stamp duty on foreign buyers and restrictions on the number of properties that can be owned by overseas investors. However, critics argue that these measures have not gone far enough, and that more needs to be done to curb the influence of international investment on London's property market.

"We need to strike a balance between attracting international investment and ensuring that Londoners can afford to live in their own city," says Stewart. "This will require a combination of measures, including building more affordable housing, regulating the private rental sector, and ensuring that international investors pay their fair share of taxes."

The future of London's luxury real estate market is uncertain, but its allure is unlikely to diminish anytime soon. The city's strong fundamentals, including its stable political system, robust legal framework, and thriving economy, will continue to attract investors from around the world. However, the challenge for London will be to manage this investment in a way that benefits the city and its residents, ensuring that London remains a vibrant and inclusive place to live, work, and invest.

CHAPTER 35: THE GREAT SMOG TO CLEAN AIR POLICIES: LONDON'S ENVIRONMENTAL LEADERSHIP

In the heart of London's history lies a chilling tale, a stark reminder of the city's past struggles with pollution. The Great Smog of 1952, a thick, acrid fog that blanketed the city for five days, brought London to a standstill and caused thousands of deaths. This environmental disaster, however, became a turning point, sparking a wave of environmental activism and policy changes that would transform London's approach to air quality and environmental protection.

The Great Smog was a toxic cocktail of smoke and fog, caused by the burning of coal for domestic heating and industrial purposes. The smog was so thick that visibility was reduced to a few meters, and public transport ground to a halt. The death toll was staggering, with an estimated 4,000 people dying in the immediate aftermath and many more suffering long-term health effects.

The Great Smog shocked the nation and galvanized public

opinion. It highlighted the dangers of pollution and the urgent need for action to improve air quality. The government responded by introducing the Clean Air Act of 1956, which introduced smokeless zones, restricted the burning of coal, and encouraged the use of cleaner fuels.

"The Great Smog was a wake-up call," says Dr. Gary Fuller, an air pollution scientist at Imperial College London. "It showed us the devastating impact that pollution can have on human health and the environment. It was a turning point that led to a fundamental shift in our approach to air quality."

The Clean Air Act of 1956 was a landmark piece of legislation, but it was just the beginning. London continued to grapple with air pollution, particularly from traffic emissions. The city introduced a Low Emission Zone in 2008, which charged high-polluting vehicles to enter central London. This was followed by the introduction of the Ultra-Low Emission Zone (ULEZ) in 2019, which expanded the area covered by the charge and tightened emission standards.

"London has been a pioneer in tackling air pollution," says Fuller. "The city's policies have been effective in reducing emissions and improving air quality. But there's still more to do, especially in tackling pollution from transport."

London's efforts to improve air quality have not been without controversy. The ULEZ, in particular, has been met with opposition from some businesses and residents who argue that it unfairly penalizes drivers and disproportionately affects low-income households. However, supporters of the ULEZ argue that it is a necessary measure to protect public health and that the benefits outweigh the costs.

"The ULEZ is not a silver bullet," says Fuller. "But it's an important tool in the fight against air pollution. It's already had a positive impact on air quality in central London, and we need to continue to expand its reach."

London's environmental leadership extends beyond air quality. The city has also made strides in reducing waste, increasing recycling, and promoting sustainable transport.

The London Plan, the city's strategic planning document, sets out ambitious targets for reducing carbon emissions and creating a more sustainable and resilient city.

"London is committed to becoming a net-zero carbon city by 2030," says Shirley Rodrigues, Deputy Mayor for Environment and Energy. "This is a challenging but achievable goal, and it will require a concerted effort from all Londoners."

The city's commitment to sustainability is evident in its many green initiatives. London has one of the largest urban tree populations in the world, and the city is investing in new parks, green spaces, and green infrastructure. London is also promoting the use of electric vehicles, with a growing network of charging points and incentives for drivers to switch to cleaner vehicles.

"London is leading the way in urban sustainability," says Rodrigues. "The city is setting an example for other cities around the world, demonstrating that it is possible to create a thriving and sustainable urban environment."

The story of London's environmental transformation is one of challenge, innovation, and resilience. The city has come a long way since the dark days of the Great Smog, but the journey is far from over. As London continues to grow and evolve, it will face new environmental challenges, such as climate change and resource scarcity. However, the city's commitment to sustainability and its track record of innovation give cause for optimism.

The future of London is green. The city is embracing a new era of environmental consciousness, with a focus on sustainable development, clean energy, and a circular economy. London's environmental leadership is a source of pride for its residents and an inspiration for other cities around the world.

CHAPTER 36: LONDON FASHION: FROM SAVILE ROW TO STREETWEAR

London's fashion landscape is a captivating tapestry woven from threads of tradition, rebellion, and innovation. From the bespoke tailoring of Savile Row to the vibrant streetwear scene of Shoreditch, the city's fashion influence reverberates across the globe. London's unique blend of historical legacy, cultural diversity, and cutting-edge creativity has cemented its position as a global fashion capital, setting trends that ripple through the industry and shape the way we dress.

The story of London fashion begins on Savile Row, a hallowed street in Mayfair renowned for its bespoke tailoring. For centuries, Savile Row has been synonymous with impeccable craftsmanship and timeless elegance. Its tailors, masters of their craft, have dressed royalty, celebrities, and discerning gentlemen from all walks of life. The suits of Savile Row, with their precise cuts, luxurious fabrics, and attention to detail, have become a global benchmark for sartorial excellence.

"Savile Row is the home of bespoke tailoring," says Anda Rowland, Vice Chairman of Anderson & Sheppard, a renowned Savile Row tailor. "It's a place where tradition and craftsmanship are valued above all else. A Savile Row suit is not just a garment; it's an investment, a symbol of quality and style."

However, London's fashion scene is not just about tradition. The city has always been a hotbed of rebellion and innovation, pushing the boundaries of fashion and challenging conventional norms. The punk movement of the 1970s,with its DIY aesthetic and anti-establishment ethos, emerged from London's streets, influencing fashion trends around the world. Vivienne Westwood, the "godmother of punk," rose to prominence during this era, her rebellious designs challenging the fashion establishment and inspiring a new generation of designers.

"London is a city that embraces individuality and creativity," says Jefferson Hack, co-founder of Dazed Media, a leading fashion and culture platform. "It's a place where new ideas and trends are born, and where the fashion industry is constantly evolving."

Today, London's fashion scene is a vibrant mix of high fashion and streetwear, established brands, and emerging talent. The city's fashion colleges, such as Central Saint Martins and the London College of Fashion, are renowned for their cutting-edge curriculum and have produced some of the industry's most influential designers, including Alexander McQueen, John Galliano, and Stella McCartney.

London Fashion Week, a biannual event showcasing the latest collections from British and international designers, is a major highlight of the global fashion calendar. The event attracts buyers, journalists, and influencers from around the world, eager to discover the next big thing in fashion.

"London Fashion Week is a celebration of creativity and diversity," says Caroline Rush, Chief Executive of the British Fashion Council. "It's a platform for emerging talent and a showcase for established brands. It's a testament to London's position as a global fashion capital."

London's fashion industry is not without its challenges. The rise of fast fashion and online retail has disrupted the traditional fashion landscape, putting pressure on smaller designers and independent retailers. The COVID-19 pandemic also had a significant impact on the industry, forcing many businesses to close their doors.

However, London's fashion scene is resilient and adaptable. Designers are embracing new technologies and business models, such as e-commerce and social media, to reach a wider audience. The city's diverse community of designers is also a source of strength, bringing fresh perspectives and innovative ideas to the industry.

"London's fashion scene is a testament to the city's resilience and creativity," says Hack. "It's a place where fashion is not just about clothes; it's about culture, identity, and self-expression. It's a place where anything is possible."

London's fashion influence is a global phenomenon, shaping trends, inspiring creativity, and driving economic growth. From the bespoke tailoring of Savile Row to the vibrant streetwear scene of Shoreditch, London's fashion landscape is a dynamic and ever-evolving tapestry. As the city continues to embrace its multicultural identity and foster innovation, its fashion scene is poised to remain a global leader for years to come.

CHAPTER 37: THE LONDON FINTECH REVOLUTION: RESHAPING GLOBAL FINANCE

The digital age is ushering in a financial revolution, and at the heart of this transformation lies London, a city at the forefront of the burgeoning fintech (financial technology) sector. Within the Square Mile and beyond, a vibrant ecosystem of innovative start-ups, established financial institutions, and tech-savvy investors is disrupting traditional banking models, revolutionizing financial services, and redefining the way we interact with money.

London's fintech scene is a testament to the city's adaptability and innovative spirit. It's a place where centuries-old financial traditions intersect with cutting-edge technology, where established banks collaborate with agile start-ups, and where a diverse range of talent converges to create a new financial landscape.

"London is a global fintech powerhouse," says Janine Hirt, CEO of Innovate Finance, a membership organisation representing the UK's fintech community. "The city's unique blend of financial expertise, regulatory support, and technological innovation makes it an ideal environment for fintech companies to thrive."

The numbers speak for themselves. London is home to over 2,500 fintech companies, employing over 100,000 people and generating billions in revenue. In 2022 alone, London's fintech sector attracted over £11 billion in investment, a testament to the global confidence in the city's fintech ecosystem.

The London fintech revolution is driven by a confluence of factors. Firstly, London's established position as a global financial centre provides a fertile ground for fintech innovation. The city's deep pool of financial expertise, its well-developed infrastructure, and its access to global markets make it an attractive destination for fintech entrepreneurs and investors.

Secondly, the UK government has been proactive in supporting the fintech sector. It has implemented a regulatory framework that encourages innovation while ensuring consumer protection. The government has also launched initiatives such as the Fintech Sandbox, which allows companies to test new products and services in a controlled environment.

Thirdly, London's diverse talent pool is a key driver of fintech innovation. The city attracts talented individuals from around the world, drawn by its vibrant culture, diverse economy, and opportunities for career advancement. This diversity of talent fuels innovation and creativity, leading to new ideas and new ways of doing business.

The impact of London's fintech revolution is far-reaching. Fintech companies are transforming the way we bank, invest, and manage our finances. They are making financial services more accessible, affordable, and convenient for consumers and businesses alike.

Take Monzo, for example, a mobile-only bank that has disrupted the traditional banking model with its user-friendly app and innovative features. Or Revolut, a digital banking platform that offers low-cost international money transfers and multi-currency accounts. These are just two examples of the many London-based fintech companies that are changing the way we think about money.

The London fintech revolution is not just about convenience and innovation; it's also about social impact. Fintech companies are using technology to address financial exclusion, providing access to financial services to those who have traditionally been underserved by the banking sector.

However, the London fintech revolution is not without its challenges. The rapid pace of technological change is disrupting traditional business models and creating new risks and uncertainties. The regulatory landscape is also constantly evolving, making it challenging for fintech companies to keep up.

"The fintech revolution is a disruptive force," says Hirt. "It's challenging the status quo and forcing traditional financial institutions to adapt or risk being left behind. But it's also creating new opportunities for growth and innovation."

The future of London's fintech scene is bright. The city's strong fundamentals, its supportive ecosystem, and its diverse talent pool are all factors that will continue to drive innovation in the fintech sector. As technology continues to evolve, London's fintech companies are poised to play an even greater role in shaping the future of finance.

London's fintech revolution is a story of innovation, disruption, and the power of technology to transform the way we interact with money. It's a story that is still being written, with new chapters unfolding every day. As London continues to evolve as a global financial centre, its fintech scene will remain a vital engine of growth, a testament to the city's enduring spirit of innovation and its ability to adapt to the changing tides of the digital age.

CHAPTER 38: CROSSRAIL: MODERNIZING LONDON'S TRANSPORT FOR THE 21ST CENTURY

Beneath the bustling streets of London, a transformation of epic proportions has taken place. The Elizabeth line, formerly known as Crossrail, has emerged as a modern marvel of engineering, a new artery that pumps life into the city's transport network. This ambitious infrastructure project, spanning over 100 kilometres (62 miles) and connecting 41 stations, is set to redefine London's transport landscape, offering faster journeys, increased capacity, and improved connectivity for millions of commuters and visitors.

The Elizabeth line is not just a new railway line; it's a symbol of London's commitment to progress and innovation. The project, which took over a decade to complete and cost £18.8 billion, is one of the largest and most complex infrastructure projects ever undertaken in Europe. It involved tunnelling under central London, constructing new stations, and upgrading existing infrastructure to create a seamless and integrated transport network.

"The Elizabeth line is a game-changer for London," says Andy Byford, London's Transport Commissioner. "It's the most significant addition to the transport network in a generation, and it will transform the way people travel around the city."

The Elizabeth line's impact on London is already evident. It has reduced journey times between key destinations, improved access to jobs and opportunities, and boosted economic growth in areas along the route. The line's spacious, air-conditioned trains and step-free access have also made travel more comfortable and accessible for passengers of all abilities.

"The Elizabeth line has already had a positive impact on London's economy and quality of life," says Byford. "It's making it easier for people to get to work, school, and leisure activities, and it's supporting the growth of businesses and communities along the route."

The Elizabeth line is not just about transport; it's about placemaking and regeneration. The new stations, designed by world-renowned architects, have become landmarks in their own right. They have also acted as catalysts for regeneration, attracting new investment and development to areas that were previously underserved by public transport.

"The Elizabeth line is more than just a transport project," says Byford. "It's a regeneration project, a placemaking project, and a project that will shape the future of London for generations to come."

The line's impact on property values is already being felt. Research by JLL, a real estate consultancy, found that properties within a 10-minute walk of an Elizabeth line station have seen their values increase by an average of 4.5% since the line's announcement. This uplift is expected to continue as the line's full benefits are realized.

The Elizabeth line is also a boon for London's tourism industry. It provides easy access to many of the city's major attractions, including Heathrow Airport, the West End, and the Olympic Park. The line's fast and frequent service makes it an attractive option for tourists who want to explore the city.

"The Elizabeth line is a fantastic asset for London's tourism industry," says Laura Citron, CEO of London & Partners, the city's official promotional agency. "It makes it easier for visitors to explore the city and discover all that London has to offer."

However, the Elizabeth line is not without its challenges. The project was delayed and over budget, and there are ongoing concerns about its long-term financial sustainability. The line's high fares have also been criticized, making it unaffordable for some passengers.

Despite these challenges, the Elizabeth line is a testament to London's ambition and its ability to deliver major infrastructure projects. The line is already transforming the way people travel around the city, and its impact is only set to grow in the years to come.

The Elizabeth line is a symbol of London's modernity and its commitment to creating a world-class transport system. It's a project that has redefined the city's connectivity, boosted its economy, and enhanced its quality of life. As London continues to evolve, the Elizabeth line will remain a vital part of its infrastructure, a testament to the city's enduring spirit of innovation and progress.

CHAPTER 39: LONDON'S GAY SCENE: FROM UNDERGROUND TO MAINSTREAM

From the clandestine clubs of Soho in the 1950s to the vibrant celebrations of Pride in London today, the evolution of London's gay scene is a story of resilience, activism, and social progress. The city's role in the global LGBTQ+ rights movement is undeniable, with London serving as a beacon of hope and a catalyst for change. This chapter explores the historical struggles, cultural contributions, and ongoing challenges that have shaped London's LGBTQ+ community and its impact on the wider world.

London's gay scene has its roots in the underground. In the mid-20th century, homosexuality was illegal in the UK, and LGBTQ+ individuals faced discrimination and persecution. Despite this, a vibrant underground scene thrived in SoHo, with clandestine bars and clubs providing a safe haven for the LGBTQ+ community.

"Soho was a place where we could be ourselves, away from the judgmental eyes of society," recalls Peter Tatchell, a veteran LGBTQ+ rights activist who has been at the forefront of the movement for over five decades. "It was a place of camaraderie, creativity, and resilience."

The Sexual Offences Act of 1967 decriminalized homosexuality in England and Wales, marking a turning point for the LGBTQ+ community. However, discrimination and prejudice persisted, and the AIDS crisis of the 1980s further marginalized the community. Despite these challenges, the LGBTQ+ community in London continued to organize and advocate for their rights, culminating in the first official Pride march in London in 1972.

Pride in London has since become one of the largest Pride events in the world, attracting hundreds of thousands of participants and spectators each year. It's a celebration of LGBTQ+ identity, a platform for activism, and a symbol of the community's resilience and progress.

"Pride is a powerful expression of our identity and our community," says Alison Camps, Co-Chair of Pride in London. "It's a time to celebrate our achievements, to raise awareness of the challenges we still face, and to demand equality and respect."

London's gay scene has made significant contributions to the city's cultural landscape. LGBTQ+ artists, writers, musicians, and performers have enriched London's cultural life, pushing boundaries and challenging norms. Soho, with its theatres, bars, and clubs, remains a vibrant hub for LGBTQ+ culture, while new queer spaces are emerging across the city.

"London's LGBTQ+ community is a source of creativity and innovation," says Dr. Justin Bengry, a historian specializing in LGBTQ+ history. "We have a long and proud history of artistic expression, and we continue to make significant contributions to the city's cultural life."

London's influence on global LGBTQ+ rights and culture is undeniable. The city has been at the forefront of the fight for equality, and its activists have inspired movements around the world. London's cultural exports, including music, film, and television, have also helped to shape global perceptions of LGBTQ+ people and issues.

"London is a global leader in LGBTQ+ rights and culture," says Tatchell. "We have a responsibility to use our platform to advocate for equality and to support LGBTQ+ people around the world."

However, London's LGBTQ+ community still faces challenges. Homophobia, transphobia, and discrimination persist, particularly in certain communities and online spaces. The recent rise in hate crimes against LGBTQ+ people is a stark reminder that the fight for equality is far from over.

"We cannot be complacent," says Camps. "We need to continue to fight for our rights, to challenge discrimination, and to create a society where everyone is free to be themselves."

The future of London's gay scene is bright. The city's LGBTQ+ community is resilient, creative, and politically engaged. With continued activism and advocacy, London can continue to be a beacon of hope for LGBTQ+ people around the world, a place where diversity is celebrated, and where everyone is free to love and live authentically.

CHAPTER 40: THE GHERKIN: ICONIC ARCHITECTURE IN THE CITY OF LONDON

In the heart of London's financial district, a towering glass edifice stands as a testament to the city's bold embrace of modern architecture. Nicknamed the Gherkin for its distinctive pickle-like shape, 30 St Mary Axe has become an iconic symbol of London's skyline, captivating locals and tourists alike. The Gherkin is more than just a building; it's a cultural touchstone, a feat of engineering, and a reflection of London's ever-evolving identity as a global city.

Designed by renowned architect Norman Foster, the Gherkin is a marvel of sustainable design and technological innovation. Its curved glass façade, comprised of 5,500 diamond-shaped panels, allows natural light to flood the interior while minimizing energy consumption. The building's aerodynamic shape reduces wind resistance, making it more stable and energy-efficient.

"The Gherkin is a masterpiece of modern architecture," says Deyan Sudjic, Director of the Design Museum in London. "It's a building that is both functional and beautiful, a testament to the power of design to transform our cities."

The Gherkin's impact on London's skyline is undeniable. Its distinctive silhouette stands out amidst the city's traditional architecture, a bold statement of London's embrace of modernity. The building has become a popular tourist attraction, with visitors flocking to its top-floor restaurant and bar for panoramic views of the city.

"The Gherkin has become an icon of London," says Murray. "It's a building that people recognize and identify with, a symbol of the city's dynamism and its willingness to embrace new ideas." The Gherkin's construction in 2004 marked a turning point in London's architectural landscape. It signalled a new era of bold and innovative designs, challenging the traditional aesthetic of the city. The Gherkin's success paved the way for other iconic buildings, such as the Shard, the Walkie Talkie, and the Cheesegrater, to rise and reshape London's skyline.

This new wave of architecture has sparked a debate about the role of modern design in shaping London's identity. Some critics argue that these tall buildings are out of scale with their surroundings, that they overshadow historic landmarks, and that they cater primarily to the wealthy elite. Others argue that they are a necessary part of London's growth and development, providing much-needed office space, housing, and amenities.

"The Gherkin is a catalyst for a broader conversation about the future of London's skyline," says Murray. "It's a building that challenges us to think about how we want our city to look and feel, and how we can balance the needs of different communities and interests."

The Gherkin is a symbol of London's economic power and its status as a global financial centre. It houses the headquarters of Swiss Re, a global reinsurance company, and other major financial institutions. The building's prime location in the heart of the City of London makes it a sought-after address for businesses seeking to project an image of modernity and success.

"The Gherkin is a symbol of London's economic vitality,"

says Chris Hayward, Policy Chairman of the City of London Corporation. "It's a building that attracts global businesses and investment, contributing to the city's prosperity."

The Gherkin's legacy extends beyond its architectural and economic significance. It has become a cultural icon, featured in films, television shows, and even video games. The building has also inspired a new generation of architects, who are pushing the boundaries of design and sustainability.

"The Gherkin is a building that will continue to inspire and amaze for generations to come," says Sudjic. "It's a testament to the power of human ingenuity and the ability to create structures that are both functional and beautiful."

The Gherkin is a microcosm of London's multifaceted identity. It's a symbol of the city's history, its modernity, its economic power, and its cultural vibrancy. It's a building that challenges us to think about the future of our cities and the role that architecture plays in shaping our lives. As London continues to evolve and grow, the Gherkin will remain a constant reminder of the city's ambition, its innovation, and its unwavering spirit of progress.

CHAPTER 41: LONDON'S STREET MARKETS: FROM BOROUGH TO PORTOBELLO

The clatter of stallholders setting up their wares, the enticing aroma of street food, the vibrant hues of fresh produce, and the symphony of haggling voices—these are the sights and sounds that define London's street markets. A quintessential part of London's identity, these bustling bazaars offer a unique blend of commerce, culture, and community. From the historic Borough Market to the eclectic Portobello Road Market, London's street markets are not just places to shop; they are living, breathing organisms that reflect the city's diversity, creativity, and entrepreneurial spirit.

London's street markets have a long and rich history, dating back centuries. In medieval times, markets were held in open spaces throughout the city, offering a wide range of goods, from food and clothing to livestock and household wares. These markets were not just places of commerce; they were also social hubs, where people gathered to exchange news, gossip, and ideas.

Today, London's street markets continue to play a vital role in the city's economy and culture. They provide a platform for small businesses and independent traders, offering a diverse range of products that are not available in mainstream retail outlets. They also attract a diverse clientele, from local residents to tourists, drawn by the markets' unique atmosphere and the opportunity to discover hidden gems.

"London's street markets are a vital part of the city's retail landscape," says David Preston, Chief Executive of the National Association of British Market Authorities. "They offer a unique shopping experience, with a focus on quality, diversity, and community."

Borough Market, located near London Bridge, is one of the city's oldest and most famous food markets. Its history dates back to the 11th century, and it has been a hub for food trade for centuries. Today, Borough Market is a foodie paradise, offering a wide range of fresh produce, artisanal cheeses, baked goods, and street food from around the world.

"Borough Market is a food lover's dream," says food writer and broadcaster Jay Rayner. "It's a place where you can find the best of British produce, as well as exotic ingredients from all over the world. It's a feast for the senses."

Portobello Road Market, located in the trendy Notting Hill neighborhood, is another iconic London market. It's famous for its antiques and vintage clothing, but it also offers a diverse range of other goods, including food, books, and music. Portobello Road Market is a popular destination for tourists and film crews, and it has been featured in numerous movies and television shows.

"Portobello Road Market is a treasure trove," says antiques dealer and TV presenter Paul Martin. "It's a place where you can find unique and unusual items, from vintage clothing and jewellery to antique furniture and collectibles."

London's street markets are not just about shopping; they are also important cultural and social spaces. They provide a platform for local artists and musicians to showcase their work, and they host a variety of events and festivals throughout the year. Markets like Brick Lane Market and

Columbia Road Flower Market are famous for their lively atmosphere and eclectic mix of stalls.

"London's street markets are more than just places to buy and sell," says Preston. "They are community hubs, where people come together to socialize, celebrate, and connect with their local heritage."

The COVID-19 pandemic has had a significant impact on London's street markets, with many traders struggling to survive during lockdowns and restrictions. However, the markets have shown remarkable resilience, adapting to the changing circumstances by offering online shopping and delivery services. As restrictions ease, the markets are bouncing back, with shoppers eager to return to the hustle and bustle of these vibrant spaces.

"London's street markets are an integral part of the city's identity," says Rayner. "They are a symbol of its diversity, its creativity, and its entrepreneurial spirit. They are a testament to the enduring power of community and the human need for connection."

London's street markets are a microcosm of the city itself, a vibrant and diverse tapestry of cultures, cuisines, and characters. They are a reminder of the city's rich history, its entrepreneurial spirit, and its unwavering commitment to community. As London continues to evolve and adapt to the challenges of the 21st century, its street markets will remain a vital part of its identity, a testament to the city's enduring appeal and its ability to reinvent itself.

CHAPTER 42: THE LONDON DESIGN FESTIVAL: SHOWCASING CREATIVE INNOVATION

The air buzzes with anticipation as designers, architects, artists, and enthusiasts from across the globe descend upon London for the annual London Design Festival (LDF). This extraordinary event transforms the city into a living gallery, showcasing cutting-edge design across various disciplines and solidifying London's position as a global leader in creative innovation.

The London Design Festival, founded in 2003, is a testament to the city's vibrant design scene. It's a celebration of creativity, ingenuity, and the power of design to shape our world. The festival spans nine days, encompassing a wide range of events, exhibitions, installations, and talks that explore the latest trends and innovations in design.

"The London Design Festival is a global showcase for creativity," says Ben Evans CBE, Director of the London Design Festival. "It's a platform for established and emerging designers to share their ideas, connect with a global audience, and drive innovation in the design industry."

LDF's influence on global design trends is undeniable. The festival has become a breeding ground for new ideas and a catalyst for creative collaborations. It attracts leading designers, manufacturers, and retailers from around the world, who come to discover the latest trends, network with industry peers, and seek out new talent.

The festival's impact extends far beyond the nine days of the event itself. It has helped to establish London as a global design hub, attracting investment, talent, and businesses to the city. The festival has also raised awareness of the importance of design in our everyday lives, inspiring a new generation of designers and consumers.

"The London Design Festival has had a profound impact on the design industry," says Evans. "It has helped to raise the profile of design, stimulate innovation, and foster collaboration between designers, manufacturers, and retailers."

London's design scene is a diverse and dynamic ecosystem, encompassing a wide range of disciplines, from architecture and product design to fashion and graphic design. The city's design schools, such as the Royal College of Art and Central Saint Martins, are renowned for their world-class programs and have produced some of the most influential designers of our time.

"London is a melting pot of creativity," says Sir John Sorrell CBE, Chairman of the London Design Festival. "It's a place where people from all over the world come together to share their ideas and their passion for design."

The London Design Festival is not just about showcasing established talent; it's also about nurturing emerging designers. The festival's Design Districts, located in various neighbourhoods throughout the city, offer a platform for up-and-coming designers to showcase their work to a wider audience. The festival's Global Design Forum, a series of talks and debates, also provides a platform for designers to discuss the challenges and opportunities facing the industry.

"The London Design Festival is a springboard for emerging talent," says Evans. "It's a place where young designers can get their work seen, connect with industry professionals, and build their careers."

The festival's commitment to diversity and inclusion is also noteworthy. It showcases designers from a wide range of backgrounds, cultures, and perspectives, reflecting the diversity of London itself. The festival also actively promotes sustainability and social responsibility, encouraging designers to consider the environmental and social impact of their work.

"The London Design Festival is committed to making design more inclusive and sustainable," says Evans. "We believe that design has the power to create a better world, and we want to ensure that everyone has the opportunity to participate in the design process."

The London Design Festival is a testament to London's enduring creativity and its ability to adapt and innovate. It's a celebration of the city's rich design heritage and its ongoing commitment to pushing the boundaries of what is possible. As London continues to evolve as a global design hub, the London Design Festival will remain a vital platform for showcasing creative innovation, inspiring new ideas, and shaping the future of design.

CHAPTER 43: LONDON'S POLISH COMMUNITY: THE LARGEST MIGRANT GROUP

Stroll through the vibrant streets of Ealing in West London, and you might hear the lively chatter of Polish conversations, catch a glimpse of red and white flags, or notice shop signs advertising pierogi and kielbasa. You're experiencing a microcosm of London's Polish community, the city's largest migrant group. This community, with its rich history, cultural traditions, and significant contributions, has woven itself into the fabric of London life, enriching the city's diversity and dynamism.

London's Polish community is not a recent phenomenon. Its roots can be traced back to the Second World War, when thousands of Polish soldiers and civilians sought refuge in the UK. After the war, many Poles decided to stay, laying the foundation for a thriving community that has continued to grow and evolve over the decades.

Today, London is home to an estimated 147,000 Polish-born residents, making them the largest foreign-born group in the city. They are concentrated in areas like Ealing, Hammersmith and Fulham, and Brent, where Polish shops, restaurants, and cultural centres cater to the community's needs.

"London's Polish community is a vibrant and dynamic part of the city," says Dr. Kasia Narkowicz, a researcher at the Polish Social and Cultural Association (POSK) in Hammersmith. "We are proud of our heritage and culture, and we are committed to contributing to the wider London community."

The impact of London's Polish community is evident in many aspects of city life. Economically, Poles have made significant contributions to the city's workforce, working in a variety of sectors, from construction and hospitality to healthcare and finance. They have also established a thriving network of businesses, from delicatessens and bakeries to construction companies and language schools.

"Polish people are known for their strong work ethic and entrepreneurial spirit," says Michael Dembinski, Chairman of POSK. "We are proud to be contributing to London's economy and creating jobs for people from all backgrounds."

Culturally, the Polish community has enriched London's cultural landscape with its unique traditions, festivals, and artistic expressions. POSK, a cultural centre established in 1963, serves as a hub for Polish culture in London, hosting events such as concerts, exhibitions, and language classes. The annual Polish Festival in Hammersmith, a celebration of Polish culture and cuisine, attracts thousands of visitors each year.

"We are committed to preserving and promoting Polish culture in London," says Dembinski. "We want to share our traditions with the wider community and build bridges between different cultures."

The Polish community is also actively engaged in civic and political life. Several Polish-born individuals have been elected to local councils and the UK Parliament, representing the interests of their constituents and advocating for policies that benefit the wider community. The Polish community is also involved in various charitable and volunteer initiatives, contributing to the social fabric of the city.

"We want to be active and engaged members of the London

community," says Narkowicz. "We believe that we have a lot to offer, and we are committed to making a positive contribution to the city."

The integration of London's Polish community has not been without its challenges. Language barriers, discrimination, and cultural misunderstandings have posed obstacles for some individuals. The Brexit referendum of 2016 also created uncertainty for many Poles living in the UK, raising concerns about their future status and rights.

"Brexit has been a difficult time for many Poles in London," says Narkowicz. "But we are resilient, and we are determined to stay and continue to contribute to the city that we have made our home."

The future of London's Polish community is intertwined with the future of London itself. As the city continues to evolve and adapt to a post-Brexit reality, the Polish community will remain an important part of its social, cultural, and economic fabric. With its strong sense of community, entrepreneurial spirit, and commitment to integration, the Polish community is poised to continue making significant contributions to London's rich tapestry of cultures.

CHAPTER 44: THE THAMES BARRIER: LONDON'S DEFENSE AGAINST CLIMATE CHANGE

A colossal feat of engineering stands guard at the mouth of the River Thames, a silent sentinel protecting London from the rising tides of climate change. The Thames Barrier, with its gleaming steel gates and imposing presence, is a testament to London's forward-thinking approach to environmental challenges and its commitment to safeguarding the city's future. This chapter delves into the history, functionality, and ongoing significance of the Thames Barrier, examining its role in mitigating flood risk and the broader implications for London's resilience in the face of climate change.

The Thames Barrier, completed in 1982, is a marvel of modern engineering. Its ten massive steel gates, each weighing over 3,000 tons, can be raised to create a temporary dam, protecting London from tidal surges that could inundate large parts of the city. The barrier has been closed over 200 times since its construction, saving London from potentially devastating floods.

"The Thames Barrier is a vital piece of infrastructure," says Steve East, Engineering Manager for the Thames Barrier. "It's a testament to the ingenuity and foresight of the engineers who designed and built it. Without the barrier, London would be much more vulnerable to flooding."

The Thames Barrier's construction was prompted by the devastating North Sea flood of 1953, which inundated parts of the UK and killed over 300 people in London alone. This disaster highlighted the vulnerability of London to flooding and the need for better protection. The Thames Barrier was designed to protect London from a 1-in-1000-year flood event, a level of protection that was considered adequate at the time. However, the impact of climate change has raised new concerns about the barrier's adequacy. Rising sea levels and more frequent extreme weather events mean that the risk of flooding is increasing. A recent study by the Environment Agency found that the Thames Barrier may need to be closed more frequently in the future to protect London from flooding.

"Climate change is a major challenge for London," says Dr. Liz Stephens, a climate scientist at the University of Reading. "The Thames Barrier is a vital defence against flooding, but it's not a panacea. We need to take a holistic approach to flood risk management, including improving natural flood defences, building resilient infrastructure, and adapting to a changing climate."

The Thames Barrier is just one part of London's multi-layered approach to flood risk management. The city has also implemented a range of other measures, such as improving river embankments, creating flood storage areas, and implementing sustainable drainage systems. The Thames Estuary 2100 Plan, a long-term strategy for managing flood risk in the Thames Estuary, is currently being updated to take into account the latest climate change projections.

"London is taking a proactive approach to flood risk management," says East. "We're constantly monitoring the situation and adapting our plans to ensure that London remains resilient in the face of climate change."

The Thames Barrier is not just a feat of engineering; it's

a symbol of London's commitment to protecting its people and infrastructure from the impacts of climate change. It's a reminder that even the most ambitious challenges can be overcome with ingenuity, collaboration, and a long-term vision.

The Thames Barrier is a testament to London's leadership in environmental protection and sustainable development. The city is at the forefront of efforts to mitigate and adapt to climate change, and its experience is being shared with other cities around the world. London's approach to flood risk management is a model for other coastal cities, demonstrating that it is possible to protect vulnerable communities and infrastructure from the rising tides.

The Thames Barrier is a symbol of hope in the face of climate change. It's a reminder that we can protect our cities and communities from the worst impacts of climate change if we act now. London's experience shows that investing in resilient infrastructure and adapting to a changing climate is not just a necessity; it's an opportunity to create a more sustainable and equitable future for all.

CHAPTER 45: LONDON'S CRAFT BEER SCENE: LEADING A GLOBAL REVOLUTION

The rich aroma of hops fills the air, a symphony of clinking glasses and lively chatter creates a vibrant atmosphere, and a diverse array of amber, golden, and dark brews entice discerning palates. Welcome to London's craft beer scene, a burgeoning landscape that has transformed the city into a global epicentre for beer innovation. From traditional pubs reimagining classic ales to cutting-edge breweries experimenting with bold new flavours, London's craft beer scene is a testament to the city's rich brewing heritage and its enduring spirit of creativity and entrepreneurship.

London's love affair with beer dates back centuries. In medieval times, ale was the drink of choice for Londoners, with pubs and breweries scattered throughout the city. The Industrial Revolution saw the rise of large-scale breweries, such as Fuller's and Young's, which produced iconic beers like London Pride and Young's Bitter. However, the dominance of mass-produced lagers in the latter half of the 20th century led to a decline in the diversity and quality of beer available in London.

The craft beer revolution, which began in the United States in the 1980s, arrived in London in the early 2000s. A new generation of brewers, inspired by the creativity and experimentation of their American counterparts, began to challenge the dominance of mass-produced lagers. These craft brewers, often operating out of small, independent breweries, focused on quality ingredients, innovative brewing techniques, and unique flavour profiles.

"London's craft beer scene is a vibrant and exciting movement," says James Watt, co-founder of BrewDog, a leading craft brewery with its roots in Scotland but a significant presence in London. "It's a community of passionate brewers who are pushing the boundaries of what beer can be."

London's craft beer scene has exploded in recent years. The city is now home to over 150 breweries, producing a wide range of beers, from traditional ales and porters to experimental IPAs and sours. Craft beer bars and pubs have also proliferated, offering a diverse selection of local and international brews.

"London has become a global destination for craft beer lovers," says Melissa Cole, a beer writer and sommelier. "The city's breweries are producing some of the most exciting and innovative beers in the world, and its bars and pubs offer a fantastic opportunity to explore the diversity of the craft beer scene."

London's craft beer scene is not just about beer; it's also about community and culture. Breweries often host taprooms and events, creating spaces where beer lovers can gather, socialize, and learn about the brewing process. Many breweries are also committed to sustainability, using locally sourced ingredients, reducing waste, and promoting responsible consumption.

"Craft beer is more than just a drink," says Watt. "It's a culture, a community, and a way of life. It's about bringing people together and celebrating the art of brewing."

The craft beer scene has also had a significant economic

impact on London. It has created jobs, boosted tourism, and revitalized local communities. The Bermondsey Beer Mile, a stretch of railway arches in South London that is home to a cluster of breweries and taprooms, has become a popular tourist destination, attracting visitors from around the world. "The craft beer scene is a major contributor to London's economy," says Cole. "It's creating jobs, supporting local businesses, and attracting investment. It's also helping to revitalize neighbourhoods and create a sense of community."

However, London's craft beer scene is not without its challenges. The high cost of operating a brewery in London can be a barrier for some businesses. The COVID-19 pandemic also had a significant impact on the industry, forcing many breweries and pubs to close temporarily.

Despite these challenges, London's craft beer scene remains resilient and optimistic. Brewers are adapting to the changing landscape, embracing new technologies and business models, such as online sales and home delivery. The community spirit that has always been a hallmark of the craft beer scene is also stronger than ever, with breweries supporting each other through these difficult times.

"The craft beer scene is a testament to the resilience and creativity of London's entrepreneurs," says Watt. "We are a community that is passionate about beer and committed to supporting each other. I believe that the future of craft beer in London is bright."

London's craft beer scene is a story of innovation, passion, and community. It's a story that is still unfolding, with new breweries, bars, and beers emerging all the time. As London continues to evolve as a global city, its craft beer scene will remain a vibrant and influential force, shaping the future of beer and contributing to the city's rich cultural tapestry.

CHAPTER 46: THE LONDON ZOO: URBAN WILDLIFE CONSERVATION

In the heart of Regent's Park, amidst the hustle and bustle of London, lies an oasis of biodiversity and conservation. The London Zoo, one of the world's oldest scientific zoos, is more than just a collection of exotic animals. It is a world-leading conservation charity, dedicated to the preservation of endangered species and their habitats. Through its research, education, and breeding programs, the London Zoo plays a vital role in global conservation efforts, inspiring future generations and raising awareness of the urgent need to protect our planet's precious wildlife.

The London Zoo's history is intertwined with the history of conservation itself. Founded in 1828 by Sir Stamford Raffles, the zoo was initially conceived as a scientific institution, a place where animals could be studied and research conducted to advance our understanding of the natural world. Over the years, the zoo's mission has evolved to encompass conservation, education, and community engagement.

"The London Zoo is a unique institution," says Dr. Andrew Terry, Director of Conservation and Policy at the Zoological Society of London (ZSL), the charity that runs the zoo. "It's a place where people can connect with wildlife, learn about conservation, and support our vital work to protect endangered species around the world."

The London Zoo's commitment to conservation is evident in its diverse range of programs and initiatives. The zoo is actively involved in field conservation projects around the world, working to protect endangered species like the Sumatran tiger, the western lowland gorilla, and the Asiatic lion. The zoo also conducts research into animal behavior, health, and genetics, contributing to our understanding of wildlife and informing conservation strategies.

"We are not just a zoo," says Terry. "We are a conservation organization with a global reach. Our work extends far beyond the zoo's walls, and we are committed to making a real difference for wildlife and people."

One of the zoo's most notable achievements is its involvement in the reintroduction of endangered species back into the wild. In 2019, the zoo successfully released a group of critically endangered mountain chicken frogs back into their native Montserrat after a captive breeding program. This project, a collaboration between ZSL, the Durrell Wildlife Conservation Trust, and the Government of Montserrat, demonstrates the power of zoos to contribute to conservation efforts.

"The London Zoo is a leader in captive breeding and reintroduction programs," says Professor Bill Sutherland, Miriam Rothschild Chair in Conservation Biology at the University of Cambridge. "Their work is helping to save some of the world's most endangered species from extinction."

The London Zoo is also a centre for education, inspiring future generations of conservationists. The zoo's education programs reach over 1 million people each year, from school children to adults. The zoo offers a variety of educational experiences, including workshops, talks, and behind-the-scenes tours, that teach visitors about animal behavior, conservation challenges, and the importance of protecting wildlife.

"The London Zoo is a place where people can learn about the natural world and be inspired to take action," says Dr.

Chris Draper, Head of Animal Welfare and Care at the Born Free Foundation, an animal welfare and conservation charity. "Education is a powerful tool for conservation, and the London Zoo is playing a vital role in educating the public about the importance of protecting our planet's wildlife."

However, the London Zoo's conservation efforts are not without challenges. The zoo faces financial constraints, competition from other attractions, and changing public attitudes towards zoos. Some animal rights activists criticize the practice of keeping animals in captivity, arguing that it is unethical and detrimental to animal welfare.

"We recognize that there are legitimate concerns about zoos," says Terry. "But we believe that modern zoos, like the London Zoo, play a vital role in conservation. We are committed to providing the highest standards of animal welfare and ensuring that our animals thrive in our care."

The London Zoo is a dynamic and evolving institution, adapting to the changing needs of conservation and society. The zoo is constantly innovating, developing new ways to engage visitors, support conservation projects, and promote sustainability. The zoo's future is bright, with a focus on research, education, and community engagement.

The London Zoo is a symbol of hope in the face of the global biodiversity crisis. It is a place where people can connect with nature, learn about conservation, and support efforts to protect our planet's precious wildlife. The zoo's legacy is one of scientific discovery, conservation impact, and educational excellence. It is a legacy that will continue to inspire and empower future generations of conservationists.

CHAPTER 47: LONDON'S INDIAN DIASPORA: FROM SOUTHALL TO THE CITY

The vibrant tapestry of London's multicultural identity is woven with threads from around the world, and the Indian diaspora forms a significant and colourful strand. From the bustling streets of Southall, often dubbed 'Little India', to the corporate boardrooms in the City, the Indian community has left an indelible mark on London's culture, economy, and social fabric. This chapter delves into the history, contributions, and evolving identity of London's Indian diaspora, showcasing its integral role in shaping the modern metropolis.

London's connection with India dates back centuries, stemming from the colonial era. However, the post-war period witnessed a significant influx of Indian immigrants, drawn by economic opportunities and the promise of a better life. They settled in various parts of London, with Southall emerging as a major hub for the Indian community.

"Southall is the heart of the British Indian community," says Dr. Pushpinder Chowdhry, MBE, Chairman of the Indian Cultural Society of the UK. "It's a place where we can connect with our roots, celebrate our traditions, and feel a sense of belonging."

The streets of Southall are a sensory overload, a kaleidoscope of sights, sounds, and smells that transport you straight to India. The air is thick with the aroma of spices, the shops are overflowing with colourful fabrics and intricate jewellery, and the sounds of Bollywood music and Punjabi bhangra fill the air. Southall's culinary scene is a particular highlight, with a wide range of restaurants and street food vendors offering authentic Indian cuisine.

"Southall is a foodie paradise," says food writer and broadcaster Anjum Anand. "It's the best place in London to experience the authentic flavours of India."

Beyond Southall, the Indian community has spread throughout London, establishing businesses, contributing to the workforce, and enriching the city's cultural scene. Indian entrepreneurs have made their mark in various sectors, from technology and finance to retail and hospitality. The city's diverse culinary scene is a testament to the Indian community's influence, with Indian restaurants ranging from Michelin-starred fine dining establishments to humble curry houses found on every high street.

"The Indian community has made a significant contribution to London's economy and culture," says Rajesh Agrawal, Deputy Mayor of London for Business. "We are proud of the entrepreneurial spirit and hard work of the Indian diaspora."

The Indian community's influence is also evident in London's vibrant cultural scene. Bollywood films are screened in cinemas across the city, Indian dance and music performances are held in theatres and community centres, and Indian festivals like Diwali and Holi are celebrated with great fanfare. The annual Diwali in London festival, held in Trafalgar Square, is a major event that attracts thousands of visitors each year.

"London's Indian community is a vibrant and dynamic part of the city's cultural landscape," says Anita Anand, broadcaster and author of *The Patient Assassin*. "We bring a rich tapestry of traditions, festivals, and artistic expressions to the city, enriching its cultural diversity."

However, the Indian diaspora in London also faces challenges. Racism and discrimination continue to be a problem for some members of the community. The model minority myth, which portrays Indians as successful and well-integrated, can also be a burden, obscuring the experiences of those who face challenges and disadvantages.

"We need to acknowledge the diversity within the Indian community," says Dr. Chowdhry. "Not all Indians are successful professionals or entrepreneurs. There are also those who face poverty, discrimination, and social exclusion."

The future of London's Indian diaspora is one of continued growth and evolution. As the community becomes more established and integrated into British society, it is also developing its own unique identity, a blend of Indian and British cultures. The second and third generations of British Indians are increasingly embracing their heritage, while also forging their own paths in a multicultural society.

"The Indian diaspora in London is a vibrant and dynamic community," says Agrawal. "We are proud of our heritage, and we are committed to making a positive contribution to the city we call home."

London's Indian diaspora is a testament to the city's ability to embrace diversity and create a welcoming environment for people from all walks of life. It's a story of resilience, adaptation, and the enduring power of culture to connect people and enrich their lives. As London continues to evolve as a global city, its Indian community will remain a vital part of its identity, a source of creativity, innovation, and social progress.

CHAPTER 48: THE LONDON AMBULANCE SERVICE: PIONEERING EMERGENCY CARE

The shrill siren of an ambulance slicing through London's traffic is a sound that instantly commands attention. It's a call for help, a signal that lives are at stake, and a reminder of the vital role played by the London Ambulance Service (LAS) in safeguarding the city's well-being. But the LAS is more than just a rapid response unit; it is a world leader in emergency medical care, constantly innovating and refining its practices to deliver the best possible outcomes for patients. Its influence reaches far beyond the streets of London, shaping global standards for pre-hospital care and inspiring emergency services worldwide.

The LAS's roots trace back to the 19th century when horse-drawn carriages transported patients to hospitals. However, the 20th century saw a dramatic transformation, with the introduction of motorized ambulances, radio communication, and advanced life-saving techniques. Today, the LAS is a sophisticated organization, utilizing cutting-edge technology and data-driven approaches to provide timely and effective care to over 8.6 million Londoners.

"The London Ambulance Service is a pioneer in pre-hospital care," says Dr. Trisha Bain, a consultant in emergency medicine at St. Mary's Hospital, London. "They have consistently pushed the boundaries of innovation, from developing new treatment protocols to implementing advanced telemedicine systems."

The LAS's impact is not just local but global. Its protocols and practices have been adopted by emergency services worldwide, setting the benchmark for pre-hospital care. For instance, the LAS's pioneering use of mechanical CPR devices has significantly improved cardiac arrest survival rates, a model that has been replicated in numerous countries.

The LAS's influence also extends to research and education. The service collaborates with academic institutions and other emergency services to conduct research and develop new treatments and technologies. It also provides training and education programs for paramedics and other healthcare professionals, sharing its expertise and experience to improve emergency care globally.

"The London Ambulance Service is a world leader in research and education," says Professor Sir Keith Porter, an expert in pre-hospital care at the University of Birmingham. "Their work has a significant impact on the development of emergency medical services worldwide."

The LAS's success is due in part to its unique operating environment. London's high population density, diverse demographics, and complex urban landscape present unique challenges for emergency services. The LAS has adapted to these challenges by developing innovative solutions, such as the use of motorcycle responders to navigate congested traffic and the deployment of specialist teams to handle major incidents.

"The London Ambulance Service is a resilient and adaptable organization," says Garrett Emmerson, Chief Executive of the

LAS. "We are constantly innovating and adapting to meet the changing needs of our patients and the city."

However, the LAS is not without its challenges. The service faces increasing demand, with the number of emergency calls rising each year. Funding constraints and staff shortages are also putting pressure on the service. The COVID-19 pandemic has further exacerbated these challenges, with the LAS experiencing unprecedented demand for its services.

Despite these challenges, the LAS remains committed to its mission of providing high-quality emergency care to the people of London. The service is continuously investing in new technologies and training to ensure that it can meet the evolving needs of its patients.

"The London Ambulance Service is a vital part of our city's infrastructure," says London Mayor Sadiq Khan. "They are our lifesavers, and we are incredibly grateful for their dedication and professionalism."

The London Ambulance Service is a testament to London's spirit of innovation and resilience. It's a story of dedicated individuals who put their lives on the line to save others, and a testament to the power of collaboration and technology to improve healthcare outcomes. As London continues to evolve as a global city, the LAS will continue to play a vital role in safeguarding the health and well-being of its residents, while also shaping the future of emergency care around the world.

CHAPTER 49: LONDON'S CYCLING REVOLUTION: TOWARDS A SUSTAINABLE CITY

A vibrant transformation is underway on London's streets, a revolution propelled not by engines, but by pedals. The city, once notorious for its traffic congestion and air pollution, is embracing cycling as a sustainable and healthy mode of transport. This shift towards two wheels is not just a trend; it's a paradigm shift, driven by a growing awareness of the environmental and health benefits of cycling, as well as a desire to create a more liveable and sustainable city.

London's cycling revolution is a testament to the city's commitment to tackling climate change and improving air quality. With its ambitious targets to reduce carbon emissions and become a net-zero city by 2030, London is leading the way in sustainable urban mobility. The city's investment in cycling infrastructure, such as dedicated cycle lanes, bike-sharing schemes, and cycle-friendly traffic signals, has made cycling safer and more accessible for all.

"Cycling is not just a mode of transport; it's a way of life," says Will Norman, London's Walking and Cycling Commissioner. "It's a healthy, sustainable, and enjoyable way to get around the city. Our goal is to make London the best big city in the world for cycling."

The numbers speak for themselves. Cycling in London has doubled in the last decade, with over 770,000 cycle journeys made daily. The city's cycle hire scheme, Santander Cycles, has become a popular mode of transport, with over 11 million hires in 2023. The city's investment in cycling infrastructure has also yielded positive results, with a significant reduction in cycling casualties and improved air quality in areas with dedicated cycle lanes.

"The data clearly shows that London's cycling revolution is working," says Norman. "We're seeing more people cycling, fewer accidents, and cleaner air. This is a win-win for everyone."

The benefits of cycling are manifold. It's a low-cost, low-carbon mode of transport that improves physical and mental health, reduces traffic congestion, and contributes to a more liveable and sustainable city. Cycling also has a positive impact on local businesses, with studies showing that cyclists spend more money in local shops than motorists.

"Cycling is good for the environment, good for our health, and good for the economy," says Norman. "It's a solution to many of the challenges facing our cities today."

London's cycling revolution is not without its challenges. The city's streets are still dominated by cars, and many cyclists feel unsafe sharing the road with motor vehicles. The lack of secure bike parking is also a barrier for many people who would like to cycle more often. The city's hilly terrain can also be a deterrent for some.

However, London is taking steps to address these challenges. The city is investing in a network of segregated cycle superhighways, which provide a safe and direct route for cyclists to travel across the city. New cycle parking facilities are being built, and the city is encouraging businesses to provide showers and changing facilities for their employees who cycle to work.

"We're working hard to make cycling safer and more accessible for everyone," says Norman. "We want to create a city where cycling is the natural choice for short journeys, and where everyone feels safe and confident on their bike."

London's cycling revolution is also inspiring other cities around the world. Cities like Paris, New York, and Amsterdam are following London's lead, investing in cycling infrastructure and promoting cycling as a sustainable mode of transport.

"London is a global leader in cycling," says Morten Kabell, CEO of the European Cyclists' Federation. "The city's commitment to cycling is an inspiration to us all. It shows that it is possible to create a world-class cycling city, even in a large and complex metropolis like London."

The London cycling revolution is a story of transformation, innovation, and the power of collective action. It's a story that is still unfolding, with new challenges and opportunities emerging all the time. As London continues to evolve as a global city, its commitment to cycling will remain a key part of its identity, a testament to the city's ambition to create a more sustainable, healthy, and liveable future for all.

CHAPTER 50: THE BRITISH LIBRARY: PRESERVING KNOWLEDGE IN THE DIGITAL AGE

In the heart of London, nestled amidst the bustling streets and historic landmarks, a modern marvel stands as a testament to the enduring power of knowledge and the relentless march of progress. The British Library, a colossal institution housing a vast collection of books, manuscripts, maps, music scores, and digital media, is more than just a library; it is a global centre for information, research, and cultural exchange. This chapter delves into the library's pivotal role in preserving and disseminating knowledge in the digital age, examining its vast collection, cutting-edge digitization efforts, and its commitment to making information accessible to all.

The British Library, founded in 1973, is a relatively young institution compared to its counterparts like the Bodleian Library in Oxford or the Bibliothèque Nationale de France. However, its collection is unparalleled in its scope and depth, encompassing over 170 million items from around the world and across millennia. The library's holdings include everything from ancient manuscripts and medieval illuminated texts to modern novels and scientific journals.

It also houses a vast collection of digital media, including websites, social media posts, and born-digital publications.

"The British Library is a treasure trove of human knowledge," says Roly Keating, Chief Executive of the British Library. "It's a place where people can come to discover the past, explore the present, and imagine the future."

The library's role in preserving knowledge has never been more critical. In an age of rapid technological change, the library is at the forefront of efforts to digitize its vast collection, ensuring that it remains accessible to future generations. The library's digitization program, one of the largest in the world, has already made millions of items available online, from medieval manuscripts to 19th-century newspapers.

"Digitization is a game-changer for libraries," says Keating. "It allows us to make our collections accessible to people around the world, regardless of their location or background. It also allows us to preserve fragile and unique items for posterity."

The British Library's digitization efforts have had a profound impact on research and education. Scholars and students from around the world can now access the library's vast resources remotely, enabling them to conduct research that would have been impossible just a few decades ago. The library's online collection also provides a valuable resource for the general public, offering access to a wealth of information on a wide range of topics.

"The British Library is a global leader in digital innovation," says Dr. Sandra Collins, Director of the National Library of Ireland. "Their work is setting a standard for other libraries around the world to follow."

However, the British Library's digital transformation has not been without its challenges. The sheer scale of the collection makes digitization a daunting task, and the library must constantly balance the need to preserve its physical collection with the demands of digital access. The library also faces questions about copyright, privacy, and the long-term preservation of digital materials.

"The digital age presents both challenges and opportunities for libraries," says Keating. "We need to find new ways to preserve and make accessible the vast amounts of information that are being created in digital form. We also need to ensure that our digital collections are accessible to future generations."

The British Library is not just a repository of knowledge; it's also a centre for research, learning, and cultural exchange. The library hosts a wide range of events and exhibitions, from literary festivals and author talks to scientific conferences and art exhibitions. The library also offers a variety of educational programs, including workshops, courses, and online resources, that cater to learners of all ages and interests.

"The British Library is a place where people can come together to learn, to be inspired, and to connect with others," says Keating. "It's a place where the past, present, and future intersect."

The British Library is a testament to London's position as a global hub for knowledge and culture. The city's diverse population, its rich history, and its thriving academic and cultural institutions make it an ideal environment for the exchange of ideas and the preservation of knowledge.

"London is a city that values knowledge and learning," says Keating. "It's a place where people from all over the world come together to share their ideas and their expertise. The British Library is a reflection of that spirit of openness and collaboration."

The British Library is a symbol of hope in an age of information overload and digital disruption. It's a reminder that knowledge is power, that libraries are essential for a democratic society, and that the preservation of our cultural heritage is a shared responsibility. The British Library's work is essential for our collective future, ensuring that the knowledge and wisdom of the past are preserved and made accessible for generations to come.

CHAPTER 51: LONDON'S SURVEILLANCE NETWORK: PRIVACY VS. SECURITY IN THE MODERN METROPOLIS

London, a city steeped in history and teeming with life, is also a city under watch. An intricate web of surveillance cameras blankets its streets, transport hubs, and public spaces, capturing the movements and activities of millions of people each day. This omnipresent surveillance network, one of the most extensive in the world, is a double-edged sword, raising profound questions about the balance between security and privacy in a modern metropolis.

In the bustling streets of Soho, as tourists snap photos of the iconic red phone booths and locals hurry to their next destination, hundreds of cameras silently record their every move. The same scene unfolds in the financial district, where CCTV cameras monitor every corner of the Square Mile, and in residential neighbourhoods, where cameras guard homes and businesses. London is a city under constant surveillance, a reality that has become increasingly normalized in the post-9/11 era.

"London is one of the most shrivelled cities in the world," says Silkie Carlo, Director of Big Brother Watch, a UK-based privacy campaign group. "The city's surveillance network is vast and intrusive, and it raises serious concerns about the erosion of privacy and civil liberties."

The proliferation of surveillance cameras in London is often justified in the name of security. In the aftermath of the 7/7 bombings in 2005, the government invested heavily in CCTV cameras, arguing that they are a vital tool for preventing and detecting crime. The cameras have indeed played a role in solving crimes, but their effectiveness in preventing crime is less clear-cut.

"Surveillance cameras can be a useful tool for law enforcement," says Professor Peter Fussey, a sociologist at the University of Essex who specializes in surveillance studies. "But their effectiveness in preventing crime is debatable. There is also the risk that they can be used for discriminatory purposes, targeting certain communities or individuals."

The impact of surveillance on privacy is a major concern for many Londoners. The constant monitoring of public spaces can create a chilling effect on freedom of expression and association. It can also lead to the normalization of surveillance and the erosion of the expectation of privacy.

"Surveillance can have a detrimental impact on our sense of freedom and autonomy," says Carlo. "It can create a climate of fear and suspicion, and it can discourage people from exercising their basic rights."

London's surveillance network is not just about CCTV cameras. The city also uses a variety of other surveillance technologies, such as facial recognition, automatic number plate recognition (ANPR), and data analytics. These technologies are increasingly being used by law enforcement and intelligence agencies to monitor and track individuals.

"The use of new surveillance technologies raises significant ethical and legal concerns," says Fussey. "We need to have a public debate about how these technologies are used and what safeguards are in place to protect our privacy."

The balance between security and privacy is a complex and contested issue. There is no easy answer, and the debate is likely to continue as technology advances and the nature of threats evolves. However, it is crucial that we have an open and honest conversation about the impact of surveillance on our society.

"We need to strike a balance between security and privacy," says Carlo. "We cannot sacrifice our fundamental rights in the name of security. We need to find ways to protect both our safety and our freedom."

London's surveillance network is a microcosm of the global debate about surveillance and privacy. The city's experience can offer valuable lessons for other cities grappling with these complex issues. It is crucial that we find ways to harness the benefits of surveillance technology while also safeguarding our fundamental rights and freedoms. The future of London, and indeed the future of all cities, depends on our ability to strike this delicate balance.

CHAPTER 52: THE LONDON RESTAURANT SCENE: A GLOBAL CULINARY CAPITAL

The tantalizing aromas wafting through the streets, a symphony of clinking cutlery and lively conversation, the explosion of flavours on every palate – this is the essence of London's vibrant restaurant scene. A culinary melting pot unlike any other, London's diverse culinary landscape boasts an impressive array of cuisines, dining experiences, and innovative culinary trends. From the Michelin-starred establishments of Mayfair to the bustling street food markets of Shoreditch, London's restaurants cater to every taste and budget, solidifying its position as a global culinary capital.

London's culinary journey is a reflection of its rich history and multiculturalism. For centuries, the city has been a crossroads of cultures, attracting immigrants from all corners of the globe. Each wave of immigration has brought with it a unique culinary heritage, enriching London's food scene with new flavours, ingredients, and techniques. From the French influence in the 18th century to the Indian and Caribbean flavours introduced in the 20th century, London's culinary identity is a fascinating amalgamation of diverse cultures.

"London is a culinary mosaic," says renowned food critic Jay Rayner. "It's a city where you can find the best of every cuisine, from traditional British fare to cutting-edge fusion dishes. The sheer variety and quality of food on offer is unparalleled."

Today, London boasts over 18,000 restaurants, offering a culinary adventure that spans the globe. You can savour authentic dim sum in Chinatown, indulge in aromatic curries in Brick Lane, sample delicate sushi in Mayfair, or relish hearty Italian pasta in Soho. London's restaurants cater to every taste and budget, from Michelin-starred fine dining establishments to casual cafes and bustling street food markets.

"London's restaurant scene is incredibly diverse and dynamic," says Grace Dent, restaurant critic for The Guardian. "There's always something new and exciting happening, whether it's a new chef opening a restaurant, a new cuisine emerging, or a new trend taking hold."

London's culinary influence extends far beyond its borders. The city is a breeding ground for culinary innovation, with chefs experimenting with new ingredients, techniques, and flavour combinations. These innovations often set global trends, influencing restaurant menus and food culture worldwide.

For example, London's street food scene has exploded in popularity in recent years, with markets like Borough Market, Maltby Street Market, and Dinerama offering a diverse range of affordable and delicious food from around the world. This trend has inspired similar markets in other cities, from New York to Tokyo.

London's restaurants are also at the forefront of sustainability, with many chefs championing locally sourced, seasonal ingredients and minimizing waste. The city's diverse culinary scene also reflects its commitment to inclusivity, with restaurants catering to a wide range of dietary requirements and cultural preferences.

However, London's restaurant scene is not without its challenges. The high cost of operating a restaurant in London, coupled with soaring rents and staff shortages, has made it difficult for many businesses to survive. The COVID-19 pandemic has also had a devastating impact on the hospitality industry, with many restaurants forced to close their doors.

Despite these challenges, London's culinary scene remains resilient and innovative. Restaurants have adapted to the pandemic by offering takeaway and delivery services, and many have embraced outdoor dining. New restaurants continue to open, and the city's food scene continues to evolve and adapt to the changing tastes and preferences of its diverse population.

"London's restaurant scene is a testament to the city's resilience and creativity," says Rayner. "It's a place where food is not just about sustenance; it's about culture, community, and connection. It's a place where people come together to share a meal and to celebrate the diversity of human experience."

London's restaurant scene is a microcosm of the city itself, a vibrant and dynamic melting pot of cultures, cuisines, and ideas. It's a place where culinary traditions from around the world are celebrated and reimagined, creating a unique and ever-evolving food culture. As London continues to evolve as a global city, its restaurant scene will undoubtedly continue to play a vital role in shaping the city's identity and enriching the lives of its residents and visitors alike.

CHAPTER 53: LONDON'S CARIBBEAN COMMUNITY: FROM WINDRUSH TO NOTTING HILL CARNIVAL

The rhythmic pulse of steel drums, the vibrant hues of feathered costumes, and the intoxicating aroma of jerk chicken filling the air—these are the sights, sounds, and smells that define Notting Hill Carnival, a vibrant celebration of Caribbean culture and a testament to the enduring influence of the Caribbean community on London's identity. This chapter delves into the history, struggles, and triumphs of London's Caribbean diaspora, tracing its journey from the Windrush generation to the present day and exploring its profound impact on the city's cultural, social, and economic landscape.

The story of London's Caribbean community begins with the arrival of the HMT Empire Windrush in 1948, carrying hundreds of Caribbean migrants who answered the call to help rebuild Britain after World War II. These pioneers, often referred to as the Windrush generation, faced discrimination and hardship but persevered, establishing a vibrant community that has since become an integral part of London's multicultural fabric.

"The Windrush generation paved the way for us," says Michael Braithwaite, a community leader and the son of Windrush immigrants. "They faced immense challenges, but their courage, resilience, and determination laid the foundation for the thriving Caribbean community we have today."

The Windrush generation and their descendants have made significant contributions to London life. They have enriched the city's culture with their music, food, and festivals, adding new flavours and rhythms to London's diverse cultural tapestry. Caribbean music genres like reggae, ska, and calypso have become part of London's soundscape, while Caribbean cuisine, with its jerk chicken, rice and peas, and curries, has become a staple of London's culinary scene.

"Caribbean culture is an integral part of London's identity," says author and broadcaster Candice Carty-Williams. "It's impossible to imagine London without the sound of steel drums, the taste of jerk chicken, or the vibrant colors of Notting Hill Carnival."

The Notting Hill Carnival, held annually over the August bank holiday weekend, is the culmination of Caribbean cultural expression in London. This vibrant street festival, with its colourful costumes, pulsating music, and mouth-watering food, attracts over a million visitors each year, making it one of the largest street festivals in the world.

"Notting Hill Carnival is a celebration of Caribbean culture and heritage," says Matthew Phillip, CEO of Notting Hill Carnival Ltd. "It's a time for our community to come together, express our creativity, and share our culture with the wider world."

Beyond its cultural contributions, the Caribbean community has also played a vital role in London's economy. Caribbean entrepreneurs have established successful businesses in various sectors, from retail and hospitality to healthcare and education. They have also made significant contributions to the city's workforce, particularly in public services like the National Health Service (NHS).

However, the Caribbean community in London also faces ongoing challenges. Systemic racism and discrimination continue to affect many individuals, limiting their opportunities and perpetuating inequalities. The Windrush scandal, which saw thousands of Caribbean migrants wrongly detained, deported, or denied legal rights, exposed the deep-rooted prejudices that still exist in British society.

"We still have a long way to go to achieve true equality," says Braithwaite. "We need to acknowledge the injustices of the past and work towards building a more inclusive and equitable society for all."

The future of London's Caribbean community is one of continued growth and evolution. The community is increasingly diverse, with new arrivals from the Caribbean and other parts of the world adding to its rich tapestry. The community is also becoming more politically engaged, advocating for its rights and demanding greater representation in decision-making processes.

"The Caribbean community in London is a force to be reckoned with," says Phillip. "We are proud of our heritage, we are determined to overcome the challenges we face, and we are committed to building a better future for ourselves and our children."

London's Caribbean community is a testament to the city's resilience, diversity, and ability to embrace different cultures. It's a story of struggle, triumph, and the enduring power of community and culture. As London continues to evolve as a global city, its Caribbean community will remain an integral part of its identity, a source of creativity, energy, and inspiration.

CHAPTER 54:
THE LONDON UNDERGROUND ART SCENE: FROM BANKSY TO PUBLIC INSTALLATIONS

Beneath the labyrinthine tunnels and bustling platforms of the London Underground, a vibrant and ever-evolving art scene thrives. From the subversive stencils of Banksy to the monumental sculptures of Henry Moore, London's underground has become a canvas for creative expression, social commentary, and urban transformation. This chapter delves into the history, diversity, and impact of London's underground art scene, exploring its role in shaping global trends in street art and public installations.

London's underground art scene is not a recent phenomenon. It has its roots in the early 20th century, when artists like Man Ray and Edward McKnight Kauffer created posters and advertisements for the London Underground, transforming the subterranean network into a gallery for graphic design. This tradition of artistic intervention continued throughout the 20th century, with artists like Eduardo Paolozzi and David

Gentleman creating murals and mosaics that adorned station walls and platforms.

"The London Underground has always been a space for artistic experimentation," says Eleanor Pinfield, Head of Art on the Underground. "It's a place where artists can reach a wide audience and engage with the public in a unique way."

The rise of street art in the late 20th century brought a new dimension to London's underground art scene. Artists like Banksy, Shepard Fairey, and Stik began using the city's walls and tunnels as their canvas, creating works that challenged authority, provoked debate, and captivated the public imagination. The anonymity and ephemerality of street art added to its allure, creating a sense of mystery and intrigue.

"Street art has democratized the art world," says Dr. Clare Melhuish, co-founder of the Shoreditch Street Art Tours. "It's taken art out of the gallery and onto the streets, making it accessible to everyone."

London's street art scene is not just about aesthetics; it's also a form of social commentary and political activism. Street artists use their work to address issues such as poverty, inequality, environmentalism, and political corruption. Banksy, in particular, has become a global icon, his satirical stencils and subversive installations sparking conversations about social justice and the role of art in society.

"Street art is a voice for the voiceless," says Melhuish. "It's a way for people to express their frustrations, their hopes, and their dreams. It's a powerful tool for social change."

London's underground art scene is not limited to street art. The city's underground stations are also home to a number of public art installations, ranging from sculptures and murals to digital displays and sound installations. These works of art enrich the commuter experience, creating a sense of place and identity for each station.

"Public art can transform a utilitarian space into a place of beauty and inspiration," says Pinfield. "It can lift our spirits, challenge our perceptions, and connect us to our communities."

One example of London's commitment to public art is the Art on the Underground program, which commissions artists to create works for the Tube network. The program has featured works by some of the most renowned artists of our time, including Yayoi Kusama, Tracey Emin, and Jeremy Deller.

London's underground art scene is a microcosm of the city's diversity and creativity. It's a place where established artists and emerging talents, traditional art forms and cutting-edge techniques, and global perspectives and local voices all come together.

The London Underground's art scene is not just about aesthetics; it's about creating a sense of place, fostering community, and promoting cultural dialogue. It's about using art to connect people, inspire creativity, and challenge the status quo.

In conclusion, London's underground art scene is a testament to the city's vibrant cultural life and its commitment to public art. It's a place where art is not just confined to galleries and museums but spills out onto the streets and into the subterranean depths of the city. As London continues to evolve as a global cultural capital, its underground art scene will remain a vital source of inspiration, creativity, and social commentary.

CHAPTER 55: LONDON'S GREEN BELT: URBAN PLANNING FOR SUSTAINABILITY

Encircling London like a verdant embrace, the Metropolitan Green Belt stands as a testament to the city's commitment to balancing urban growth with environmental preservation. This sprawling swathe of protected countryside, fields, and woodlands serves as a bulwark against urban sprawl, a haven for wildlife, and a vital green lung for the capital. This chapter delves into the history, significance, and ongoing debates surrounding London's Green Belt, exploring how this innovative planning concept has shaped the city's development and contributed to its sustainability.

Established in 1947, the Green Belt is a ring of protected land surrounding London, designed to prevent urban sprawl and preserve the countryside. It covers an area of over 5,000 square kilometres (1,930 square miles), encompassing parts of Greater London, Surrey, Kent, Essex, Hertfordshire, and Buckinghamshire. The Green Belt is not just a geographical designation; it's a philosophy of urban planning that recognizes the importance of green spaces for the health and well-being of both people and the environment.

"The Green Belt is a vital part of London's identity," says Neil Sinden, Director of CPRE London, the countryside charity. "It's a green lung for the city, a haven for wildlife, and a place where people can escape the hustle and bustle of urban life."

The Green Belt's impact on London's development is undeniable. It has prevented the city from sprawling outwards, encouraging the intensification of development within existing urban areas. This has helped to protect the countryside, preserve biodiversity, and create a more compact and sustainable city.

"The Green Belt has played a crucial role in shaping London's urban form," says Professor Michael Batty, Chair of Urban Planning at University College London (UCL). "It has encouraged the development of a polycentric city, with multiple centres of activity and a more even distribution of population and jobs."

The Green Belt also provides numerous benefits for Londoners. It offers a place to escape the city's noise and pollution, providing opportunities for recreation, relaxation, and exercise. The Green Belt is also home to a diverse range of wildlife, including rare and protected species. It plays a crucial role in mitigating the effects of climate change, absorbing carbon dioxide, reducing flood risk, and regulating temperatures.

"The Green Belt is a vital green infrastructure asset for London," says Sinden. "It provides a range of environmental benefits, including clean air, flood protection, and carbon sequestration. It's also a valuable recreational resource for Londoners."

However, the Green Belt is not without its controversies. As London's population continues to grow and the demand for housing increases, there is pressure to release Green Belt land for development. Some argue that the Green Belt is an outdated concept that stifles economic growth and exacerbates the housing crisis. Others argue that it is a vital safeguard against urban sprawl and the destruction of the countryside.

"The Green Belt is a complex issue," says Batty. "There are legitimate arguments on both sides. But I believe that we need to find a way to balance the need for housing with the need to protect the Green Belt. We need to find innovative solutions that allow us to build more homes without sacrificing our green spaces."

The Mayor of London has committed to protecting the Green Belt, but has also acknowledged the need to build more homes. The London Plan, the city's strategic planning document, sets out a target of building 66,000 new homes each year, with a focus on brownfield sites and densification within existing urban areas. However, some argue that this is not enough to meet the city's housing needs, and that some Green Belt land will need to be released for development.

"The Green Belt is a finite resource," says Sinden. "We need to use it wisely and sparingly. We need to prioritize the development of brownfield sites and find ways to make our existing urban areas more liveable and sustainable."

The future of London's Green Belt is uncertain. The pressures of population growth and the demand for housing are likely to continue, and the debate over the Green Belt's future will no doubt intensify. However, the Green Belt remains a powerful symbol of London's commitment to sustainability and its recognition of the importance of green spaces for the health and well-being of its residents. The challenge for London is to find a way to balance the need for growth with the need to protect the Green Belt, ensuring that the city remains a vibrant, sustainable, and liveable place for generations to come.

CHAPTER 56: THE LONDON SCHOOL OF HYGIENE & TROPICAL MEDICINE: GLOBAL HEALTH LEADERSHIP

Within the quiet Bloomsbury district, a stone's throw away from the bustling British Museum, lies an institution that has quietly shaped global health for over a century. The London School of Hygiene & Tropical Medicine (LSHTM), with its unassuming façade, is a powerhouse of research, education, and advocacy in the field of public and global health. This chapter delves into LSHTM's pioneering contributions to global health research and policy, exploring its historical significance, current initiatives, and future aspirations in tackling the world's most pressing health challenges.

LSHTM's story began in 1899, amidst a global landscape ravaged by infectious diseases. Founded to address the health challenges of the British Empire, the school quickly established itself as a leader in tropical medicine and public health. Its early research on diseases like malaria, cholera, and tuberculosis paved the way for life-saving interventions and control strategies.

"LSHTM has a long and distinguished history of tackling global health challenges," says Professor Liam Smeeth, Dean of the Faculty of Public Health and Policy at LSHTM. "From its early days fighting infectious diseases in the tropics to its current work on non-communicable diseases, health systems strengthening, and climate change, the school has always been at the forefront of public health research and innovation."

Today, LSHTM is a world-renowned institution, attracting students and faculty from over 100 countries. The school offers a wide range of undergraduate and postgraduate programs in public health, epidemiology, infectious diseases, and health policy. Its research covers a broad spectrum of global health issues, from the prevention and control of infectious diseases to the impact of climate change on health.

"LSHTM is a truly global institution," says Smeeth. "Our students and faculty come from all over the world, and our research addresses global health challenges that affect people everywhere."

LSHTM's research has had a profound impact on global health policy and practice. The school's work on malaria control, for example, has informed the development of global strategies to combat the disease, saving millions of lives. LSHTM's research on HIV/AIDS has led to new treatments and prevention strategies, while its work on tuberculosis has helped to reduce the burden of this deadly disease.

"LSHTM's research is making a real difference in the world," says Dr. Peter Piot, Director of the London School of Hygiene & Tropical Medicine from 1995 to 2008 and a leading figure in the fight against HIV/AIDS. "Their work is not just academic; it's translating into real-world impact, improving the lives of millions of people around the globe."

LSHTM is also a leader in global health advocacy, working to influence policy and practice at the national and international levels. The school's faculty and alumni are active in a wide range of organizations, from the World Health Organization to Médecins Sans Frontières, using their expertise to advocate for better health for all.

"LSHTM is not just a research institution; it's a voice for

the voiceless," says Smeeth. "We are committed to using our research and expertise to advocate for policies that promote health equity and social justice."

Looking to the future, LSHTM is well-positioned to continue its leadership in global health. The school is investing in new research areas, such as antimicrobial resistance, digital health, and planetary health, and it is expanding its collaborations with partners around the world. LSHTM is also committed to training the next generation of global health leaders, equipping them with the knowledge and skills to tackle the complex health challenges of the 21st century.

"The future of global health is bright," says Smeeth. "We have the tools and the knowledge to address the world's most pressing health challenges. But it will require a concerted effort from all stakeholders, from governments and international organizations to researchers, healthcare workers, and communities."

The London School of Hygiene & Tropical Medicine is a beacon of hope in a world grappling with complex health challenges. Its legacy of research, education, and advocacy has saved countless lives and improved the health of millions. As London continues to evolve as a global city, LSHTM will remain a vital contributor to its international standing, a testament to the city's commitment to science, innovation, and the pursuit of a healthier world.

CHAPTER 57: LONDON'S COFFEE CULTURE: FROM TRADITIONAL CAFÉS TO THIRD WAVE COFFEE

The aroma of freshly roasted coffee beans fills the air, a symphony of grinding, steaming, and pouring creates a comforting soundtrack, and a diverse array of latte art adorns cups held by eager patrons. This sensory experience is the hallmark of London's thriving coffee culture, a dynamic scene that has transformed the city into a global hub for coffee innovation and appreciation. From the historic coffee houses of the 17th century to the cutting-edge micro-roasteries of today, London's coffee scene is a testament to the city's rich history, diverse culture, and unwavering pursuit of quality and taste.

London's love affair with coffee began in the 17th century when the first coffee houses opened their doors, offering a space for social interaction, intellectual debate, and, of course, the consumption of the newly popular beverage. These early coffee houses, such as Lloyd's Coffee House, which would later become the famous insurance market, played a pivotal role in the city's economic and social development.

"Coffee houses were the social networks of their time," says historian Matthew Green. "They were places where people from all walks of life could come together to discuss the latest news, exchange ideas, and conduct business."

The tradition of coffee drinking in London continued to evolve over the centuries, with the arrival of Italian espresso bars in the 20th century introducing a new style of coffee consumption. However, it wasn't until the emergence of the "third wave" coffee movement in the early 2000s that London's coffee scene truly began to flourish.

The third wave coffee movement is characterized by a focus on quality, craftsmanship, and ethical sourcing. It emphasizes the importance of the entire coffee production chain, from the farmer who grows the beans to the barista who prepares the final cup. This movement has transformed coffee from a commodity into a craft, with coffee connoisseurs seeking out unique flavour profiles and brewing methods.

"London is at the forefront of the third wave coffee movement," says James Hoffmann, co-founder of Square Mile Coffee Roasters and a leading figure in the UK coffee industry. "The city's coffee scene is incredibly diverse and innovative, with a focus on quality, sustainability, and ethical sourcing."

London's coffee culture is not just about the quality of the coffee; it's also about the experience. Independent coffee shops, with their cozy interiors, knowledgeable baristas, and focus on community, have become an integral part of London life. These shops offer a respite from the hustle and bustle of the city, a place to relax, socialize, and enjoy a meticulously crafted cup of coffee.

"London's coffee shops are more than just places to grab a caffeine fix," says coffee blogger and influencer Chloe Nattrass. "They are community hubs, social spaces, and creative incubators. They are a reflection of the city's unique character and its passion for quality and craftsmanship."

London's coffee scene is constantly evolving, with new trends and innovations emerging all the time. Specialty coffee shops are experimenting with new brewing methods, such as pour-over and cold brew, while roasters are sourcing beans from new origins and experimenting with different roasting profiles. The city's coffee scene is also becoming more inclusive, with a growing number of cafes catering to a diverse range of dietary needs and preferences.

"London's coffee scene is a never-ending source of inspiration," says Hoffmann. "There's always something new and exciting to discover, whether it's a new cafe, a new roast, or a new brewing method."

London's influence on global coffee trends is undeniable. The city's coffee shops and roasters have inspired a new generation of coffee entrepreneurs around the world. The city's emphasis on quality, sustainability, and ethical sourcing has also raised the bar for the entire coffee industry.

"London is setting the standard for coffee culture," says Nattrass. "The city's coffee scene is a model for other cities to follow, demonstrating that coffee can be more than just a beverage; it can be an experience, a community, and a catalyst for positive change."

London's coffee culture is a reflection of the city's rich history, diverse culture, and innovative spirit. It's a place where coffee is not just a drink; it's a passion, a lifestyle, and a celebration of quality and craftsmanship. As London continues to evolve as a global city, its coffee scene will continue to flourish, inspiring new trends and shaping the future of coffee around the world.

CHAPTER 58: THE LONDON FILM INDUSTRY: FROM PINEWOOD STUDIOS TO INDEPENDENT CINEMA

The whirl of cameras, the hushed whispers on set, and the flickering lights of the silver screen – this is the vibrant world of London's film industry. From the grand studios of Pinewood to the independent cinemas of Soho, London's celluloid landscape is a tapestry of creativity, innovation, and global influence. This chapter delves into London's cinematic legacy, exploring its historical significance, current trends, and its impact on global film production and culture.

London's love affair with cinema began in the early 20th century, with the emergence of the first film studios in the city. These studios, such as Ealing Studios and Gainsborough Pictures, produced some of the most iconic British films of all time, from comedies like *Passport to Pimlico* and *The Lavender Hill Mob* to dramas like *Kind Hearts and Coronets* and *The Ladykillers.*

The post-war era saw the rise of Pinewood Studios, a sprawling complex located just outside London in Buckinghamshire. Pinewood quickly became a major player in the global film industry, hosting the production of blockbuster films like the James Bond franchise, *Star Wars*, and the *Harry Potter* series.

"Pinewood Studios is a national treasure," says Amanda Nevill CBE, former CEO of the British Film Institute (BFI). "It's a place where film history is made, where creativity flourishes, and where British talent shines on the world stage."

Today, London's film industry is a thriving ecosystem, encompassing everything from major studios to independent production companies, from world-renowned actors and directors to cutting-edge visual effects companies. The city's film schools, such as the National Film and Television School and the London Film School, are renowned for their world-class training programs and have produced some of the industry's most talented filmmakers.

"London is a global hub for film production," says Adrian Wootton OBE, Chief Executive of Film London and the British Film Commission. "The city's diverse locations, its world-class talent pool, and its generous tax incentives make it an attractive destination for filmmakers from around the world."

London's film industry is not just about big-budget blockbusters. The city is also a hotbed for independent cinema, with a thriving network of independent cinemas, film festivals, and production companies. The British Film Institute (BFI), a cultural charity that champions British film, plays a crucial role in supporting independent filmmaking through funding, distribution, and exhibition initiatives.

"London is a city that celebrates independent cinema," says Mia Bays, Director of the BFI Film Fund. "We are committed to supporting filmmakers who are telling diverse and challenging stories, and we believe that independent cinema is essential for a vibrant and healthy film culture."

London's film industry is a significant contributor to the UK economy. In 2022, the UK film industry contributed £6.27 billion to the economy and supported over 220,000 jobs.

London itself is estimated to account for over 60% of the UK's film and television production.

However, London's film industry also faces challenges. The rising cost of production and the competition from other global film centres, such as Los Angeles and Vancouver, are putting pressure on the industry. Brexit has also created uncertainty for the sector, particularly around funding and access to European markets.

"The film industry is facing a period of unprecedented change," says Wootton. "But London is a resilient city, and we are confident that our film industry will continue to thrive."

The future of London's film industry is bright. The city's diverse talent pool, world-class infrastructure, and supportive government policies are all factors that will continue to attract filmmakers from around the world. London's film industry is also embracing new technologies, such as virtual production and artificial intelligence, which are transforming the way films are made.

"London's film industry is constantly evolving," says Bays. "We're embracing new technologies, new ways of working, and new ways of telling stories. We're a city that is always looking to the future."

London's film industry is a reflection of the city's creativity, diversity, and global outlook. It's a place where stories are told, dreams are realized, and the world is captured on film. As London continues to evolve as a global cultural capital, its film industry will remain a vital contributor to its identity and its influence on the world stage.

CHAPTER 59: LONDON'S CYBER SECURITY HUB: PROTECTING THE DIGITAL ECONOMY

In the digital age, where information is currency and cyber threats loom large, London has emerged as a formidable fortress, safeguarding the digital realm. A global cyber security hub, the city is at the forefront of combating cybercrime, protecting critical infrastructure, and fostering innovation in cyber defence. This chapter delves into the multifaceted landscape of London's cyber security sector, examining its evolution, key players, and its crucial role in protecting the digital economy, both in the UK and globally.

London's rise as a cyber security hub is a testament to its unique blend of strengths. The city's robust financial sector, with its concentration of banks, insurance companies, and fintech firms, has made it a prime target for cyberattacks. However, this vulnerability has also spurred the development of a sophisticated cyber security ecosystem, with a multitude of companies, organizations, and government agencies working together to combat cyber threats.

"London is a natural hub for cyber security," says Ciaran Martin, former CEO of the National Cyber Security Centre

(NCSC), the UK's technical authority on cyber security. "The city's concentration of financial institutions and critical infrastructure makes it a prime target for cyberattacks, but it also means that there is a strong demand for cyber security expertise and services."

London's cyber security sector is diverse and dynamic, encompassing a wide range of activities, from threat intelligence and incident response to security consulting and product development. The city is home to some of the world's leading cyber security companies, such as Darktrace, Sophos, and NCC Group, as well as a thriving community of start-ups and scaleups.

"London's cyber security sector is a hotbed of innovation," says Poppy Gustafsson, CEO of Darktrace. "We are constantly developing new technologies and approaches to address the ever-evolving threat landscape."

The UK government has played a key role in fostering the growth of London's cyber security hub. The NCSC, established in 2016, is a world-leading authority on cyber security, providing guidance and support to businesses, government agencies, and individuals. The government has also invested heavily in cyber security research and development, creating a vibrant ecosystem of academic institutions, research centres, and industry partners.

"The UK government is committed to making the UK the safest place to live and work online," says Martin. "We are investing in cyber security to protect our critical national infrastructure, our businesses, and our citizens."

London's cyber security sector is not just about defence; it's also about innovation. The city is home to a growing number of cyber security start-ups, developing cutting-edge technologies that are transforming the way we protect ourselves from cyber threats. For example, companies like Onfido are using artificial intelligence and machine learning to develop advanced identity verification solutions, while others like Tessian are using behavioral analytics to prevent email-based attacks.

"London's cyber security start-ups are at the forefront of innovation," says Gustafsson. "They are developing new technologies that are not only protecting us from cyber threats but also creating new opportunities for growth and development."

The economic impact of London's cyber security sector is significant. The sector is estimated to be worth over £8 billion and employs over 43,000 people. The sector is also growing rapidly, with demand for cyber security skills and services outstripping supply.

"The cyber security sector is a major contributor to the UK economy," says Martin. "It's a high-growth sector with a bright future."

However, London's cyber security hub also faces challenges. The shortage of skilled cyber security professionals is a major concern, as is the constantly evolving nature of cyber threats. The UK's withdrawal from the European Union has also created uncertainty for the sector, particularly around data protection and access to talent.

"The cyber security landscape is constantly changing," says Gustafsson. "We need to be agile and adaptable to stay ahead of the threats. We also need to invest in developing the next generation of cyber security talent."

London's cyber security hub is a testament to the city's resilience, innovation, and global leadership. It's a place where the best minds in the industry come together to tackle the challenges of the digital age. As technology continues to advance, London's cyber security sector is poised to play an even greater role in protecting the digital economy and ensuring the safety and security of our online world.

CHAPTER 60: THE CHANGING FACE OF LONDON'S DOCKLANDS: FROM SHIPPING TO SKYSCRAPERS

The skyline of London's Docklands is a testament to the transformative power of urban regeneration. Once a bustling hub of maritime trade, the Docklands fell into decline in the mid-20th century, leaving behind a landscape of derelict warehouses, abandoned docks, and crumbling infrastructure. However, a bold vision for the future, combined with strategic planning and substantial investment, has breathed new life into the area. Today, the Docklands stands as a thriving business district, a testament to London's adaptability and its ability to reinvent itself in the face of economic change.

The story of the Docklands' transformation begins in the 1980s, when the London Docklands Development Corporation (LDDC) was established to spearhead the regeneration efforts. The LDDC's vision was to create a new financial district that would rival the City of London, attracting international businesses and investment to the area. This ambitious plan involved a massive overhaul of the existing infrastructure, including the construction of new roads, bridges, and transport links.

The centrepiece of the redevelopment was Canary Wharf, a 97-acre site that was transformed into a gleaming cluster of skyscrapers, housing offices, shops, restaurants, and residential apartments. The development of Canary Wharf was a catalyst for further regeneration in the Docklands, attracting more businesses, residents, and visitors to the area.

"The transformation of the Docklands is a remarkable story of urban regeneration," says Eric Sorensen, Chief Executive Officer of the Canary Wharf Group. "It's a testament to the vision, determination, and collaboration of all those involved in this ambitious project."

The economic impact of the Docklands' regeneration has been significant. The area now contributes over £11 billion to the UK economy annually and employs over 120,000 people. The development of Canary Wharf has made London a more attractive destination for international businesses, helping to solidify its position as a global financial centre.

The Docklands' transformation has also had a social impact, creating new jobs and opportunities for local residents. The development has brought a mix of housing options to the area, including affordable housing, attracting a diverse range of residents and creating a more vibrant and inclusive community.

"The Docklands is a thriving and diverse community," says Jules Pipe CBE, Deputy Mayor for Planning, Regeneration and Skills. "It's a place where people from all walks of life come together to live, work, and play. It's a testament to the power of urban regeneration to create thriving communities."

However, the Docklands' regeneration has not been without its critics. Some argue that the focus on commercial development has led to a lack of affordable housing and social amenities, while others raise concerns about the environmental impact of the high-rise buildings.

"The Docklands' regeneration has been a success in many ways, but it's important to acknowledge that it has also had some negative consequences," says Dr. Penny Bernstock, a researcher at the University of East London. "We need to learn from the past and ensure that future regeneration projects are more inclusive and sustainable."

The Docklands' transformation is an ongoing process. The area continues to evolve, with new developments underway, such as the Wood Wharf project, which aims to create a new mixed-use neighborhood with a focus on sustainability and community. The Docklands Light Railway (DLR), a driverless light rail system that opened in 1987, has played a crucial role in connecting the Docklands to the rest of London, and further transport improvements are planned, including the extension of the Elizabeth line.

"The Docklands is a constantly evolving landscape," says Sorensen. "We're committed to creating a sustainable and inclusive community that benefits everyone."

The transformation of London's Docklands is a story of vision, ambition, and resilience. It's a testament to the power of urban regeneration to transform neglected areas into thriving hubs of activity. The Docklands' success has not only revitalized a part of London but also served as a model for other cities around the world grappling with the challenges of post-industrial decline. As London continues to evolve as a global city, the Docklands will remain a testament to its ability to adapt and innovate, a symbol of its enduring spirit and its commitment to creating a better future for all.

CHAPTER 61: LONDON'S CHINESE COMMUNITY: FROM LIMEHOUSE TO MODERN INTEGRATION

The aroma of roast duck wafts through the air, mingling with the chatter of Mandarin, Cantonese, and English. Red lanterns sway gently in the breeze, casting a warm glow on the bustling streets. This is Chinatown, a vibrant enclave in the heart of London that is home to the city's Chinese community. However, London's Chinese diaspora extends far beyond this iconic neighborhood, encompassing a rich tapestry of cultures, histories, and contributions that have shaped the city's identity for over two centuries. This chapter delves into the fascinating journey of London's Chinese community, from its humble beginnings in Limehouse to its modern-day integration and influence.

The story of London's Chinese community begins in the late 18th century when Chinese sailors and merchants arrived in the city, drawn by trade opportunities with the East India Company. They settled in Limehouse, a dockside area in the

East End, creating a small but vibrant community. These early settlers faced discrimination and hardship, but they persevered, establishing businesses, places of worship, and community organizations.

"Limehouse was the cradle of London's Chinese community," says Dr. Yung-Chen Lu, a historian specializing in Chinese migration to Britain. "It was a place where Chinese culture took root and began to flourish in a foreign land."

The 20th century saw a significant increase in the Chinese population in London, driven by factors such as political upheaval in China and the easing of immigration restrictions in the UK. New waves of immigrants arrived from Hong Kong, Malaysia, and other parts of Southeast Asia, bringing with them a diversity of cultures, languages, and culinary traditions.

"The Chinese community in London is incredibly diverse," says Simon Cheng, a community leader and the founder of the Chinese Community Centre in Birmingham. "We come from different parts of China and Southeast Asia, speak different dialects, and have different cultural practices. But we are united by our shared heritage and our commitment to building a better future for ourselves and our children."

The Chinese community has made significant contributions to London's economy, culture, and society. Chinese entrepreneurs have established successful businesses in a variety of sectors, from restaurants and takeaways to import-export firms and technology companies. The city's Chinatown has become a major tourist attraction, drawing millions of visitors each year and contributing to the local economy.

"The Chinese community is a vital part of London's economy," says Dr. Lu. "We create jobs, pay taxes, and contribute to the city's cultural vibrancy."

Culturally, the Chinese community has enriched London's diverse tapestry with its unique traditions, festivals, and artistic expressions. Chinese New Year celebrations in Trafalgar Square are a highlight of the city's cultural calendar, attracting thousands of spectators. The annual Dragon Boat Festival on the River Thames is another popular event, showcasing the community's rich cultural heritage.

"We are proud of our culture and heritage," says Cheng. "We want to share it with the wider community and build bridges between different cultures."

The Chinese community has also made significant contributions to London's civic and political life. Chinese-born individuals have been elected to local councils and the UK Parliament, representing the interests of their constituents and advocating for policies that benefit the wider community. The community is also involved in various charitable and volunteer initiatives, contributing to the social fabric of the city.

However, the Chinese community in London also faces challenges. Racism and discrimination remain persistent issues, exacerbated by the COVID-19 pandemic, which has seen a rise in anti-Asian hate crimes. The community also grapples with issues of identity, integration, and the balance between tradition and modernity.

"We need to address the challenges facing our community," says Cheng. "We need to fight against racism and discrimination, promote cultural understanding, and ensure that our voices are heard."

Despite these challenges, London's Chinese community remains a vibrant and resilient force. It is a community that is proud of its heritage, committed to its future, and determined to make a positive contribution to the city it calls home.

The future of London's Chinese community is intertwined with the future of London itself. As the city continues to evolve as a global hub, the Chinese community will play an increasingly important role in its economic, cultural, and social development. The community's rich heritage, entrepreneurial spirit, and commitment to integration make it a valuable asset to London, enriching the city's diversity and contributing to its continued success.

CHAPTER 62: THE LONDON MARATHON: CHARITY, COMMUNITY, AND GLOBAL HEALTH

The rhythmic pounding of tens of thousands of feet, the roar of the crowds, and the kaleidoscope of colors as runners in whimsical costumes pass by - this is the London Marathon, a global phenomenon that transcends sport. The London Marathon is more than just a race; it's a carnival of community spirit, a fundraising powerhouse for countless charities, and a catalyst for global health awareness and action. This chapter delves into the multifaceted impact of this iconic event, exploring its profound influence on philanthropy, community building, and the promotion of a healthy lifestyle worldwide.

The London Marathon's impact on philanthropy is nothing short of extraordinary. Since its inception in 1981, the event has raised over £1 billion for charitable causes, making it the largest single-day fundraising event on the planet. Each year, tens of thousands of runners take to the streets, raising money for a wide range of charities, from cancer research and mental health support to poverty alleviation and environmental conservation. The marathon has become a platform for individuals to make a difference, transforming their personal challenge into a collective force for good.

"The London Marathon is a phenomenon," says Catherine Anderson, Head of Events at Cancer Research UK, one of the marathon's official charity partners. "It's an incredible event that brings people together from all walks of life, united by a common goal of raising money for causes they care about."

The marathon's fundraising success is a testament to the generosity and spirit of the British public. It's also a reflection of the event's unique ability to inspire and motivate people to take on a personal challenge for a greater cause. The marathon's official charity partners, which include some of the UK's most well-known charities, play a crucial role in harnessing this collective energy and channelling it towards meaningful change.

"The London Marathon is a platform for hope," says Anderson. "It gives people the opportunity to make a real difference in the lives of others. It's a reminder that we can achieve great things when we come together."

Beyond philanthropy, the London Marathon has a profound impact on community building. The event brings together people from all walks of life, regardless of age, background, or ability. The sense of camaraderie and shared purpose among the runners, spectators, and volunteers is palpable, creating a unique atmosphere of unity and celebration.

The marathon's impact extends beyond race day. Many runners continue to train and participate in other events, fostering a culture of health and fitness in their communities. The marathon has also inspired a new generation of runners, with many citing the event as their motivation to take up the sport.

"The London Marathon is a catalyst for community building and a celebration of human spirit," says Brasher. "It's an event that inspires people to challenge themselves, to push their limits, and to come together for a common cause."

The London Marathon's influence also extends to global health. The event has raised awareness of the importance of physical activity and healthy living, inspiring people around the world to get active and improve their health. The marathon's extensive media coverage has also highlighted the challenges faced by communities around the world, raising awareness and mobilizing support for global health initiatives.

"The London Marathon is a global platform for promoting health and well-being," says Dr. Clare Gerada, former Chair of the Royal College of General Practitioners. "It's an event that inspires people to take care of their health and to support others in their journey towards a healthier lifestyle."

The London Marathon is a unique and powerful event that has transformed the landscape of philanthropy, community building, and global health. It's a testament to the human spirit, the power of collective action, and the enduring appeal of sport. As the marathon continues to evolve, it will undoubtedly continue to inspire, motivate, and make a positive impact on the world.

CHAPTER 63: LONDON'S ARTIFICIAL INTELLIGENCE SCENE: SHAPING THE FUTURE OF TECH

In the heart of London, amidst the city's historic landmarks and bustling financial district, a technological revolution is unfolding. A vibrant ecosystem of artificial intelligence (AI) companies, researchers, and investors is pushing the boundaries of innovation, transforming industries, and redefining the way we live and work. This chapter delves into London's burgeoning AI scene, exploring its historical roots, current landscape, and its potential to shape the future of technology on a global scale.

London's affinity for AI is not a recent phenomenon. The city's intellectual heritage, dating back to the pioneering work of Alan Turing and his code-breaking team at Bletchley Park during World War II, laid the foundation for the development of computer science and artificial intelligence. Today, London is home to world-class universities and research institutions, such as the Alan Turing Institute and DeepMind, that are at the forefront of AI research and development.

"London is a global hub for AI talent," says Tabitha Goldstaub, Co-Founder of CognitionX, an AI advice platform. "The city's strong academic base, diverse talent pool, and supportive government policies have created a fertile ground for AI innovation."

The numbers speak for themselves. London is home to over 1,300 AI companies, employing over 50,000 people and generating billions of pounds in revenue. In 2023, London attracted over £3 billion in AI investment, more than any other European city. The city's AI scene is diverse and dynamic, encompassing a wide range of sectors, from healthcare and finance to transportation and retail.

"London's AI ecosystem is one of the most vibrant and diverse in the world," says Dom Hallas, Executive Director of Coadec, a policy advocacy group for start-ups and scaleups. "The city's strength lies in its ability to attract and retain top talent, its collaborative culture, and its access to global markets."

The London AI scene is not just about research and development; it's also about commercialization and real-world impact. London-based AI companies are developing ground-breaking technologies that are transforming industries and improving lives. For example, DeepMind's AlphaFold algorithm has revolutionized protein folding prediction, a breakthrough that has the potential to accelerate drug discovery and revolutionize healthcare.

"London's AI companies are at the forefront of solving some of the world's most pressing challenges," says Goldstaub."From healthcare to climate change, AI has the potential to transform our lives for the better."

London's AI scene is also characterized by a strong focus on ethics and responsibility. The city is home to several organizations, such as the Ada Lovelace Institute and the Centre for Data Ethics and Innovation, that are dedicated to ensuring that AI is developed and used in a way that benefits society.

"AI is a powerful technology, but it also raises important ethical questions," says Hallas. "London is leading the way in ensuring that AI is developed and used responsibly, with a focus on transparency, accountability, and fairness."

However, London's AI scene is not without its challenges. The rapid pace of technological change is creating new ethical and regulatory challenges. The shortage of skilled AI talent is also a concern, as is the need for greater diversity and inclusion in the sector.

"The AI revolution is happening fast," says Goldstaub. "We need to make sure that we are prepared for the challenges and opportunities that it presents. We need to ensure that AI is developed and used in a way that benefits everyone."

The future of London's AI scene is bright. The city's strong foundations, its supportive ecosystem, and its diverse talent pool are all factors that will continue to drive innovation in the AI sector. As AI continues to evolve, London is well-positioned to remain a global leader, shaping the future of technology and using AI to create a better world.

CHAPTER 64: THE CHANGING THAMES: FROM INDUSTRIAL ARTERY TO LEISURE DESTINATION

The River Thames, a serpentine ribbon of water winding through the heart of London, has always been a vital force in shaping the city's identity. From its early days as a Roman settlement to its current status as a global metropolis, the Thames has served as a lifeline for London, a source of sustenance, transport, and inspiration. Yet, the river's role has undergone a remarkable transformation in the modern era. Once a bustling industrial artery, the Thames has evolved into a hub for leisure, recreation, and cultural activity. This chapter explores the evolving role of the Thames in London's economy and culture, examining the factors that have driven this transformation and the implications for the city's future.

In the 19th century, the Thames was the engine room of the Industrial Revolution, powering factories, transporting goods, and fuelling London's economic growth. The riverbanks were lined with docks, warehouses, and shipyards, creating a thriving industrial landscape. However, this industrial activity came at a cost. The Thames became heavily polluted, its waters choked with sewage and industrial waste.

"The Thames was a polluted mess," recalls Sir Peter Bazalgette, Chair of the Thames Estuary Partnership. "It was a symbol of the industrial age, but also a reminder of the environmental damage that we were inflicting on our planet."

The decline of heavy industry in the mid-20th century, coupled with growing environmental awareness, led to a major clean-up effort. The Thames Water Ring Main, a 130-kilometer (80-mile) network of sewers, was completed in 1994,significantly reducing the amount of sewage discharged into the river. Stricter environmental regulations were also introduced, forcing industries to clean up their act.

"The clean-up of the Thames was a remarkable achievement," says Bazalgette. "It shows what can be done when we work together to tackle environmental challenges."

Today, the Thames is a much cleaner and healthier river. Fish and other wildlife have returned to its waters, and the riverbanks have been transformed into public spaces and cultural attractions. The Thames Path, a 294-kilometer (183-mile) National Trail, offers walkers and cyclists a unique way to experience the river's beauty and diversity. The river is also a popular destination for boating, kayaking, and paddleboarding.

"The Thames is a playground for Londoners," says Merlin Fulcher, CEO of Tideway, the company responsible for the construction of the Thames Tideway Tunnel, a major infrastructure project that will further reduce sewage pollution in the river. "It's a place where people can come to relax, have fun, and connect with nature."

The Thames has also become a cultural hub. The South Bank, home to the National Theatre, the Tate Modern, and the London Eye, is a vibrant cultural quarter that attracts millions of visitors each year. The river also hosts a variety of events and festivals, such as the Totally Thames Festival and the Henley Royal Regatta.

"The Thames is a cultural artery," says Justine Simons OBE, Deputy Mayor for Culture and Creative Industries. "It's a place where creativity flourishes, where artists are inspired, and where Londoners come together to celebrate their city."

The economic impact of the Thames is still significant. The river remains an important transport artery, carrying goods and passengers to and from London. The Port of London, although much smaller than it once was, still handles over 45 million tons of cargo each year. The Thames is also home to a thriving tourism industry, with river cruises, boat trips, and riverside attractions generating significant revenue for the city.

"The Thames is a vital economic asset for London," says Bazalgette. "It's a source of jobs, investment, and tourism. It's also a symbol of London's resilience and its ability to adapt to change."

The future of the Thames is bright. The river is becoming cleaner and healthier, and its role as a leisure destination and cultural hub is only set to grow. The Thames Tideway Tunnel, when completed in 2025, will further reduce sewage pollution and improve the river's water quality. New developments along the riverbanks, such as the Nine Elms regeneration project, are also transforming the Thames into a more vibrant and sustainable environment.

"The Thames is a river with a rich history and a bright future," says Fulcher. "It's a symbol of London's resilience and its ability to reinvent itself. I believe that the Thames will continue to play a vital role in the city's life for centuries to come."

The transformation of the Thames from an industrial artery to a leisure destination is a remarkable story of environmental recovery and urban renewal. It's a testament to London's ability to adapt to change and to create a more sustainable and liveable city. As London continues to evolve, the Thames will remain a vital part of its identity, a source of inspiration, recreation, and economic opportunity.

CHAPTER 65: LONDON'S NIGERIAN COMMUNITY: INFLUENCE AND INTEGRATION

A vibrant celebration of color, music, and dance erupts in the streets of Peckham, pulsating with the rhythms of Afrobeat and the aroma of jollof rice. This is the annual Nigerian Independence Day parade, a testament to the thriving Nigerian community that has made London its home. From the bustling markets of Peckham to the corridors of power in Westminster, the Nigerian diaspora has woven itself into the fabric of London life, enriching the city's cultural diversity and contributing to its economic and social vibrancy.

London's Nigerian community is a dynamic and multifaceted group, encompassing individuals from various ethnic, religious, and socioeconomic backgrounds. Their stories are as diverse as Nigeria itself, a nation of over 200 million people and 250 ethnic groups. Some came as students seeking education, others as professionals seeking career opportunities, and many as families seeking a better life for their children.

"The Nigerian community in London is a microcosm of Nigeria itself," says Dr. Nkem Thompson, a sociologist specializing in

African diaspora studies at the University of East London. "It's a diverse and complex community, with a rich cultural heritage and a strong sense of identity."

The impact of the Nigerian community on London's social fabric is undeniable. Nigerian culture, with its vibrant music, fashion, and cuisine, has permeated London life. Afrobeat, a genre of music pioneered by Nigerian legend Fela Kuti, has become a global phenomenon, with London serving as a major hub for its production and consumption. Nigerian fashion designers, such as Duro Olowu and Nkwo Onwuka, have gained international recognition for their bold and innovative designs. Nigerian cuisine, with its flavourful stews, soups, and snacks, has also found a home in London, with Nigerian restaurants and takeaways popping up across the city.

"Nigerian culture is vibrant, energetic, and full of life," says Yemisi Aribisala, a Nigerian food writer based in London. "It's a celebration of color, flavour, and community. It's a culture that is making its mark on London and the world."

The Nigerian community has also made significant contributions to London's economy. Nigerian entrepreneurs have established successful businesses in various sectors, from technology and finance to retail and hospitality. Many Nigerians are also highly skilled professionals, working in fields such as medicine, law, and engineering.

"Nigerians are ambitious, hard-working, and resourceful," says Abike Dabiri-Erewa, Chairman/CEO of the Nigerians in Diaspora Commission (NIDCOM). "We are making a significant contribution to the UK economy and society."

The Nigerian community is also actively engaged in civic and political life in London. Nigerian-born individuals have been elected to local councils and the UK Parliament, representing the interests of their constituents and advocating for policies that benefit the wider community. The community is also involved in various charitable and volunteer initiatives, supporting vulnerable groups and promoting social cohesion.

"We are proud to be Londoners," says Dr. Thompson. "We want

to be part of the solution to the challenges facing our city. We believe that we have a lot to offer, and we are committed to making a positive contribution to London life."

However, the Nigerian community in London also faces challenges. Racism and discrimination are still prevalent, and many Nigerians feel that they are not fully accepted by British society. The Windrush scandal, which saw many long-term UK residents from Caribbean countries wrongly detained, deported, or denied legal rights, has also had a chilling effect on the wider immigrant community.

"We need to address the issue of racism and discrimination in London," says Dabiri-Erewa. "We need to create a society where everyone feels welcome and valued, regardless of their background or ethnicity."

The future of London's Nigerian community is bright. The community is young, dynamic, and full of potential. With its strong cultural identity, entrepreneurial spirit, and commitment to social justice, the Nigerian community is poised to continue making a significant impact on London's social, cultural, and economic landscape.

London's Nigerian community is a testament to the city's diversity and its ability to integrate different cultures. It's a story of resilience, adaptation, and the enduring power of culture to connect people and enrich their lives. As London continues to evolve as a global city, its Nigerian community will undoubtedly remain a vital part of its identity, a source of creativity, innovation, and social progress.

CHAPTER 66: THE LONDON FASHION AND TEXTILE MUSEUM: PRESERVING DESIGN HERITAGE

Nestled in the heart of Bermondsey Village, a vibrant creative hub in southeast London, lies a vibrant institution dedicated to showcasing the artistry and innovation of fashion and textiles. The Fashion and Textile Museum, with its striking pink and orange façade, is a testament to London's enduring influence on global fashion history. This chapter delves into the museum's role in documenting and celebrating design heritage, examining its diverse collections, engaging exhibitions, and commitment to education and research.

The Fashion and Textile Museum (FTM), founded in 2003 by iconic British designer Dame Zandra Rhodes, is a unique institution dedicated solely to contemporary fashion and textile design. Its bold and colourful building, designed by Mexican architect Ricardo Legorreta, is a landmark in its own right, reflecting the vibrancy and creativity of the museum's contents.

"The Fashion and Textile Museum is a place where fashion comes alive," says Celia Joicey, Head of the Fashion and Textile Museum. "It's a place where we can celebrate the creativity and artistry of fashion and textiles, and explore their cultural and social significance."

The museum's collection spans a wide range of fashion and textile design, from the avant-garde creations of Zandra Rhodes herself to the cutting-edge work of contemporary designers. The museum's exhibitions explore a diverse range of themes, from the history of fashion to the impact of technology on design.

"Our exhibitions are designed to be engaging and thought-provoking," says Joicey. "We want to inspire our visitors to think about fashion and textiles in new ways, and to appreciate their cultural and social significance."

The FTM's influence extends far beyond its walls. The museum plays a crucial role in documenting and preserving fashion history, ensuring that the stories of designers, makers, and wearers are not forgotten. The museum's archives and collections are a valuable resource for researchers, students, and anyone interested in the history of fashion.

"The Fashion and Textile Museum is a vital repository of fashion history," says Dr. Rebecca Arnold, Senior Lecturer in History of Dress and Textiles at the Courtauld Institute of Art. "Its collections and exhibitions provide a unique insight into the evolution of fashion and its impact on society."

The FTM is also committed to education and outreach. The museum offers a range of educational programs, workshops, and lectures, aimed at inspiring the next generation of fashion and textile designers. The museum also works with schools and community groups to promote an understanding and appreciation of fashion and textiles.

"We believe that fashion and textiles are for everyone," says Joicey. "We want to make our museum accessible to as wide an audience as possible, and to inspire people of all ages and backgrounds to engage with fashion and textiles."

London's role in documenting and influencing global fashion history is undeniable. The city has been a centre of fashion innovation for centuries, from the bespoke tailoring of Savile Row to the punk movement of the 1970s. London's fashion colleges, such as Central Saint Martins and the London College of Fashion, are world-renowned for their creative and innovative approach to fashion education.

"London is a global fashion capital," says Caroline Rush, Chief Executive of the British Fashion Council. "It's a place where trends are set, where creativity flourishes, and where the future of fashion is being shaped."

The Fashion and Textile Museum is a microcosm of London's fashion scene, reflecting its diversity, creativity, and global influence. The museum's collections, exhibitions, and educational programs provide a unique insight into the history and future of fashion, making it a must-visit destination for anyone interested in this fascinating and ever-evolving field.

As London continues to evolve as a global fashion hub, the Fashion and Textile Museum will play an increasingly important role in documenting and preserving the city's rich design heritage. The museum's commitment to education, research, and public engagement will ensure that the stories of London's fashion and textile designers continue to inspire and inform future generations.

CHAPTER 67: LONDON'S URBAN FARMING MOVEMENT: SUSTAINABILITY IN THE CITY

Amidst the towering skyscrapers and concrete jungle of London, a quiet revolution is taking root. A burgeoning urban farming movement is transforming rooftops, balconies, and derelict spaces into vibrant oases of green, where fruits, vegetables, and herbs flourish. This chapter explores London's growing embrace of urban agriculture, examining its impact on food security, community building, and the city's quest for a more sustainable future.

London's urban farming movement is not a new phenomenon. Historically, the city boasted extensive market gardens and allotments, providing fresh produce for its inhabitants. However, the Industrial Revolution and the subsequent urban sprawl led to the decline of urban agriculture. In recent years, a renewed interest in local food production, coupled with concerns about food security and environmental sustainability, has sparked a resurgence of urban farming in

London.

"Urban farming is more than just a trend; it's a necessity," says Julie Brown, founder of Growing Communities, a social enterprise that supports urban farms and community gardens in London. "It's about reconnecting people with food, building resilient communities, and creating a more sustainable food system."

London's urban farms are as diverse as the city itself. They range from rooftop gardens and hydroponic systems to community allotments and aquaponic farms. Some farms focus on providing fresh produce to local residents, while others prioritize education and community engagement. The common thread that unites them is a commitment to sustainable food production and the creation of a more resilient and equitable food system.

"Urban farming is not just about growing food; it's about creating social and environmental value," says Brown. "It's about building community, improving health and well-being, and reducing our carbon footprint."

The benefits of urban farming are manifold. It increases access to fresh, healthy, and locally grown food, reducing reliance on imported produce and strengthening local food economies. Urban farms also provide green spaces in dense urban areas, improving air quality, reducing the urban heat island effect, and promoting biodiversity. They also serve as educational hubs, teaching people about food production, sustainability, and the importance of connecting with nature.

"Urban farming is a win-win for everyone," says Chris Collins, a sustainability expert and author of *The Edible City*. "It's good for our health, good for the environment, and good for our communities."

The London urban farming movement is not without its challenges. Limited space, high land values, and the need for specialized knowledge and skills can be barriers to entry for aspiring urban farmers. The lack of a comprehensive regulatory framework for urban agriculture can also create uncertainty and hinder investment.

"Urban farming is still in its early stages in London," says Collins. "We need to create a supportive policy environment that encourages innovation and investment in urban agriculture."

Despite these challenges, London's urban farming movement is gaining momentum. The city's government has recognized the potential of urban agriculture to contribute to food security, sustainability, and community development. The London Food Strategy, a roadmap for creating a more sustainable and resilient food system for the city, identifies urban farming as a key priority.

"Urban farming has a crucial role to play in creating a more sustainable and resilient food system for London," says Deputy Mayor for Environment and Energy, Shirley Rodrigues. "We are committed to supporting the growth of urban agriculture and creating a more equitable food system for all Londoners."

The London urban farming movement is a testament to the city's creativity, resilience, and commitment to sustainability. It's a story of individuals and communities coming together to create a more just and sustainable food system. As London continues to evolve as a global city, its urban farming movement will play an increasingly important role in shaping its future, ensuring that the city has access to fresh, healthy, and locally grown food, while also building resilient communities and creating a more sustainable environment for all.

CHAPTER 68: THE LONDON SYMPHONY ORCHESTRA: CLASSICAL MUSIC IN THE MODERN AGE

In the heart of London's cultural scene, amidst the historic theatres and bustling art galleries, a symphony of sound echoes through the grand concert halls. This is the home of the London Symphony Orchestra (LSO), a world-renowned ensemble that has been a driving force in the world of classical music for over a century. The LSO's story is not just about the harmonious notes it produces, but also about London's pivotal role in shaping global classical music trends, nurturing talent, and preserving a rich musical heritage.

The LSO, founded in 1904, has a rich and storied history. From its early days performing in Queen's Hall to its current residency at the Barbican Centre, the LSO has consistently pushed the boundaries of classical music, collaborating with renowned composers and conductors, premiering ground-breaking works, and championing musical education and outreach.

"The LSO is a musical institution of global renown," says Sir Simon Rattle, Music Director of the LSO from 2017-2023."It's an orchestra with a rich history and a bright future, and it's an integral part of London's cultural landscape."

London's influence on global classical music trends is undeniable. The city has long been a magnet for musical talent, attracting composers, conductors, and performers from around the world. London's concert halls, including the Barbican Centre, the Royal Festival Hall, and the Wigmore Hall, are renowned for their acoustics and their diverse programming, offering a rich variety of classical music experiences.

"London is a global music capital," says Kathryn McDowell CBE, Managing Director of the LSO. "It's a place where musical traditions from around the world converge, and where new and exciting sounds are constantly being created."

The LSO's impact on the classical music world extends far beyond its performances. The orchestra is a pioneer in music education and outreach, offering programs that reach diverse audiences, from young children to adults. The LSO Discovery program, for example, provides opportunities for people of all ages and abilities to engage with classical music through workshops, masterclasses, and interactive performances.

"The LSO is committed to making classical music accessible to everyone," says McDowell. "We believe that music has the power to transform lives, and we want to share that power with as many people as possible."

The LSO has also embraced technology to expand its reach and engage new audiences. The orchestra's digital platform, SO Play, offers live and on-demand streaming of concerts, interviews, and educational content. The LSO also collaborates with digital artists and technologists to create immersive and interactive musical experiences.

"Technology is opening up new possibilities for classical music," says McDowell. "It's allowing us to reach new audiences, experiment with new formats, and create new ways for people to experience music."

However, London's classical music scene is not without its challenges. The high cost of tickets and the perception of classical music as elitist can make it inaccessible to some audiences. The COVID-19 pandemic has also had a devastating impact on the performing arts, with concert halls forced to close and orchestras facing financial difficulties.

"The classical music industry is facing a period of uncertainty," says McDowell. "But we are resilient, and we are determined to find new ways to connect with our audiences and ensure that classical music continues to thrive."

The future of London's classical music scene is one of innovation and adaptation. Orchestras like the LSO are experimenting with new formats, such as outdoor concerts and digital performances, to reach wider audiences. They are also embracing diversity and inclusion, commissioning works by composers from underrepresented backgrounds and creating programs that appeal to a broad range of tastes and interests.

"The future of classical music is bright," says Rattle. "It's a living tradition that is constantly evolving and adapting. It's a music that speaks to the human condition and has the power to move, inspire, and unite us."

The London Symphony Orchestra is a testament to London's enduring love of music and its commitment to artistic excellence. It's a symbol of the city's cultural vibrancy, its global outlook, and its unwavering support for creativity and innovation. As London continues to evolve as a global cultural capital, the LSO will remain a vital part of its identity, a beacon of musical excellence, and a source of inspiration for generations to come.

CHAPTER 69: LONDON'S BIOTECH INDUSTRY: PIONEERING MEDICAL INNOVATIONS

In the bustling heart of London, amidst the historic landmarks and vibrant cultural scene, a revolution is brewing in the field of biotechnology. London has emerged as a global leader in this cutting-edge industry, fostering innovation, attracting top talent, and pushing the boundaries of scientific discovery. This chapter delves into the multifaceted landscape of London's biotech scene, examining its historical context, current progress, and its potential to transform the future of healthcare and medicine.

London's prowess in biotechnology is not a recent development. The city boasts a long and illustrious history of scientific innovation, from the pioneering work of Alexander Fleming, who discovered penicillin at St. Mary's Hospital in 1928, to the ground-breaking research conducted at institutions like the Francis Crick Institute and Imperial College London. This rich scientific heritage has laid the foundation for London's current status as a global biotech hub. "London has a unique combination of factors that make it an ideal location for biotech innovation," says Dr. Malcolm Weir, CEO of the Medicines Discovery Catapult, a UK government-funded initiative to accelerate drug discovery. "The city has world-class universities, research institutions, and a thriving life sciences ecosystem. It also benefits from a supportive government and a diverse talent pool."

The numbers speak for themselves. London is home to over 1,000 biotech companies, employing over 25,000 people and generating billions of pounds in revenue. In 2023, London attracted over £1 billion in venture capital investment for biotech, surpassing Paris and Berlin to become the leading biotech hub in Europe.

London's biotech scene is diverse and dynamic, encompassing a wide range of subsectors, from drug discovery and development to medical devices and diagnostics. The city's companies are working on ground-breaking therapies for diseases like cancer, Alzheimer's, and rare genetic disorders. They are also developing innovative medical devices, such as wearable health monitors and robotic surgical systems.

"London's biotech companies are at the forefront of medical innovation," says Dr. Menelas Pangalos, Executive Vice President of BioPharmaceuticals R&D at AstraZeneca, a leading global pharmaceutical company with a major presence in London. "They are developing new treatments and technologies that have the potential to transform healthcare and improve the lives of millions of people around the world."

London's biotech ecosystem is supported by a robust infrastructure that includes world-class research institutions, such as the Francis Crick Institute and the Wellcome Sanger Institute, as well as a network of incubators, accelerators, and co-working spaces. The city also benefits from a supportive regulatory environment and a strong intellectual property regime.

However, London's biotech scene is not without its challenges.

The high cost of research and development, the lengthy regulatory approval process for new drugs and devices, and the competition from other global biotech hubs, such as Boston and San Francisco, are all significant hurdles.

Despite these challenges, London's biotech industry is thriving. The city's strengths, including its talent pool, diverse ecosystem, and supportive government, continue to attract investment and innovation. London's biotech companies are also forging strategic partnerships with global pharmaceutical companies and academic institutions, accelerating the development and commercialization of new therapies and technologies.

"London's biotech scene is a collaborative and innovative ecosystem," says Professor Sir Paul Nurse, Nobel laureate and Director of the Francis Crick Institute. "We are working together to translate cutting-edge science into new treatments and cures for diseases."

Looking ahead, London's biotech industry is poised for continued growth and innovation. The city's commitment to research and development, its supportive ecosystem, and its diverse talent pool are all factors that will drive the next wave of medical breakthroughs. London's biotech companies are not just developing new drugs and devices; they are creating a new paradigm for healthcare, one that is more personalized, precise, and effective.

London's biotech industry is a beacon of hope in a world grappling with complex health challenges. It is a testament to the power of human ingenuity, the importance of scientific discovery, and the potential of collaboration to improve human health. As London continues to evolve as a global city, its biotech scene will remain a vital engine of growth, a source of medical innovation, and a symbol of the city's commitment to a healthier and more sustainable future.

CHAPTER 70:
THE CHANGING FACE OF SOHO:
FROM BOHEMIA TO BUSINESS

The neon lights flicker, casting a kaleidoscopic glow on the cobblestone streets. The air is thick with the aroma of international cuisine, mingled with the faint scent of history. Laughter and music spill out from bustling pubs and bars, while crowds of theatregoers emerge from the iconic venues of the West End. This is Soho, a neighborhood that has been a pulsating heart of London life for centuries. Yet, Soho is not a static entity; it is a place of constant evolution and transformation. This chapter explores the fascinating metamorphosis of Soho, from its bohemian roots to its current status as a bustling commercial hub, examining the forces that have shaped its identity and the challenges it faces in maintaining its unique character.

Soho's history is a tapestry woven with threads of counterculture, creativity, and transgression. In the 18th and 19th centuries, Soho was a notorious district, known for its brothels, gambling dens, and seedy establishments. However, it also attracted artists, writers, and musicians, drawn by its affordability and bohemian spirit.

The 20th century saw Soho become a centre for London's LGBTQ+ community, with numerous gay bars and clubs springing up in the area. Soho also became a hub for the music and film industries, with iconic venues like the 2i's Coffee Bar and the Marquee Club hosting legendary performances by the likes of The Rolling Stones, David Bowie, and Jimi Hendrix.

"Soho has always been a place of diversity and rebellion," says Dan Carrier, a local historian and author of *The History of Soho*. "It's a place where people have come to express themselves, to challenge the norms, and to find their tribe."

In recent decades, Soho has undergone a dramatic transformation. The sex industry has largely disappeared, replaced by upscale restaurants, trendy bars, and media companies. The area has become a magnet for tourists, drawn by its vibrant nightlife, diverse culinary scene, and cultural offerings.

"Soho has gentrified," says Carrier. "The old Soho of sex shops and strip clubs is largely gone. It's been replaced by a more sanitized, commercialized version of itself."

This transformation has brought economic prosperity to Soho, but it has also sparked concerns about the loss of its bohemian character and cultural identity. Some long-time residents and businesses have been priced out of the area, and there are fears that Soho is losing its unique charm.

"Soho is at a crossroads," says Tim Lord, Chief Executive of Soho Estates, a property company that owns a large part of Soho. "We need to find a way to balance the needs of businesses and residents, to preserve the area's heritage, and to ensure that Soho remains a vibrant and diverse place for everyone."

The challenges facing Soho are not unique. Many historic neighbourhoods around the world are grappling with the forces of gentrification and commercialization. The key is to find a way to embrace change while still preserving the character and identity that make these places special.

"Soho's future depends on its ability to adapt and evolve," says Carrier. "It needs to find new ways to support its creative community, to preserve its historic buildings, and to create spaces that are accessible to everyone."

There are signs that Soho is rising to this challenge. The Soho Society, a community organization, is actively involved in protecting the area's heritage and promoting its unique character. New initiatives, such as the Soho Create Festival, are showcasing the work of local artists and designers.

"Soho is still a vibrant and creative place," says Lord. "It's home to a diverse community of people who are passionate about the area. We are committed to working with them to ensure that Soho remains a special place for generations to come."

The story of Soho is a microcosm of London's evolution as a global city. It's a story of change, adaptation, and the ongoing struggle to balance economic growth with cultural preservation. Soho's future is uncertain, but its past and present provide a rich tapestry of stories, characters, and experiences that continue to captivate and inspire. As London continues to evolve, Soho will remain a vital part of its identity, a testament to the city's diversity, creativity, and resilience.

CHAPTER 71: LONDON'S BENGALI COMMUNITY: FROM BRICK LANE TO MAINSTREAM

The tantalizing aroma of curry spices fills the air, mingling with the rhythmic beats of Bengali music. Colourful saris and vibrant fabrics adorn shop windows, while the lively chatter of Sylheti and Bengali fills the streets. Welcome to Brick Lane, the heart of London's Bengali community. This vibrant enclave in the East End is a testament to the enduring legacy of the Bangladeshi diaspora, whose rich culture, resilience, and entrepreneurial spirit have left an indelible mark on London's identity.

London's connection with the Bengali community began in the mid-20th century, when immigrants from the Sylhet region of Bangladesh (then East Pakistan) arrived in the city, seeking economic opportunities and a better life. They settled in the East End, drawn by its affordable housing and proximity to the docks, where many found employment.

The 1970s saw a surge in Bangladeshi immigration due to political instability and natural disasters in Bangladesh. Brick Lane, with its affordable rent and proximity to the garment industry, became a hub for the burgeoning community.

Bengali businesses, such as curry houses and clothing shops, sprang up along the street, creating a unique cultural enclave that became known as "Banglatown."

"Brick Lane is more than just a street," says Ansar Ahmed Ullah, a community leader and the founder of the Brick Lane Circle, a local community organization. "It's a symbol of our community's resilience and our contribution to London."

The Bengali community has had a profound impact on London's cultural landscape. Bengali cuisine, with its fragrant curries, flavourful biryanis, and unique sweets, has become a beloved part of London's food scene. Brick Lane, with its countless curry houses, is a culinary destination for both locals and tourists.

"Brick Lane is the curry capital of the UK," says chef and food writer Asma Khan, owner of the renowned Darjeeling Express restaurant. "It's a place where you can experience the authentic flavours of Bengali cuisine."

Beyond food, the Bengali community has also enriched London's cultural life with its music, art, and literature. The annual Boishakhi Mela, a Bengali New Year celebration held in Brick Lane, is a major cultural event that attracts thousands of visitors. Bengali artists and writers, such as Monica Ali and Zia Haider Rahman, have gained international recognition for their contributions to literature.

"Bengali culture is rich and diverse," says Shamim Azad, a poet and playwright. "It's a culture that celebrates storytelling, music, and the arts. It's a culture that is making its mark on London and the world."

The Bengali community has also made significant contributions to London's economy. Bangladeshi entrepreneurs have established successful businesses in various sectors, from retail and hospitality to technology and finance. The community is also a major employer in the city, with Bangladeshis working in a wide range of industries.

"The Bengali community is a vital part of London's economy," says Rushanara Ali, MP for Bethnal Green and Bow. "We are hard-working, entrepreneurial, and committed to building a better future for ourselves and our children."

However, the Bengali community in London also faces challenges. Poverty, discrimination, and social exclusion remain significant issues for many Bangladeshis. The community also grapples with issues of identity, integration, and the preservation of its cultural heritage in a rapidly changing city.

"We need to address the challenges facing our community," says Ullah. "We need to tackle poverty, fight discrimination, and ensure that our young people have the opportunities they need to succeed."

The future of London's Bengali community is one of hope and optimism. The community is young, dynamic, and full of potential. With its strong cultural identity, entrepreneurial spirit, and commitment to social justice, the Bengali community is poised to continue making significant contributions to London's diverse tapestry.

The Bengali community is an integral part of London's identity, a vibrant and dynamic force that has enriched the city's culture, economy, and social fabric. It's a story of resilience, adaptation, and the enduring power of culture to connect people and build bridges across communities. As London continues to evolve as a global city, its Bengali community will undoubtedly remain a vital part of its identity, a testament to the city's diversity and its ability to embrace different cultures.

CHAPTER 72: THE LONDON WETLAND CENTRE: URBAN CONSERVATION IN ACTION

In the southwestern corner of London, a surprising oasis of tranquillity and biodiversity flourishes amidst the urban sprawl. The London Wetland Centre, a 105-acre wetland reserve managed by the Wildfowl & Wetlands Trust (WWT), is a testament to London's commitment to urban conservation. This chapter delves into the significance of this urban wetland, exploring its role in preserving biodiversity, providing educational opportunities, and fostering a connection between Londoners and the natural world.

The London Wetland Centre, opened in 2000, is a remarkable example of urban revitalization. The site was once a collection of derelict Victorian reservoirs, abandoned and neglected. Through a visionary project led by the WWT, the reservoirs were transformed into a thriving wetland habitat, home to a diverse array of birds, insects, amphibians, and mammals.

"The London Wetland Centre is a shining example of what can be achieved when we work to restore nature in urban environments," says Martin Senior, Chief Executive of the WWT. "It's a place where people can reconnect with nature, learn about the importance of wetlands, and support our vital conservation work."

The Centre's impact on local biodiversity is undeniable. It provides a safe haven for a wide range of wildlife, including over 200 species of birds, such as the elusive bittern and the colourful kingfisher. The wetlands also support a variety of invertebrates, fish, and amphibians, contributing to the ecological health of the region.

"The London Wetland Centre is a biodiversity hotspot," says Dr. Mike Maunder, Director of the WWT London Wetland Centre. "It's a place where nature thrives, and it's a vital resource for scientific research and conservation education."

The Centre's educational programs are another important aspect of its work. It welcomes over 200,000 visitors each year, including school groups, families, and birdwatchers. The Centre offers a range of educational activities, from guided walks and talks to pond dipping and birdwatching workshops. These programs aim to inspire a love of nature and raise awareness of the importance of wetland conservation.

"The London Wetland Centre is a place where people of all ages can learn about the natural world and be inspired to take action to protect it," says Maunder. "Education is a key part of our mission, and we are committed to providing engaging and informative learning experiences for all our visitors."

The Centre's success is not just about its environmental and educational impact; it's also about its contribution to the local community. The Centre is a popular destination for local residents, providing a peaceful escape from the hustle and bustle of city life. It also hosts a range of community events, such as nature-themed workshops and family activities.

"The London Wetland Centre is a valuable community asset," says Sarah Perry, a local resident and regular visitor to the Centre. "It's a place where we can connect with nature, relax, and enjoy the outdoors. It's also a great place to meet other people who share our passion for wildlife."

The London Wetland Centre is a model for urban conservation, demonstrating how nature can be integrated into our cities to create healthier, more sustainable, and more liveable environments. Its success has inspired similar projects around the world, and it is a testament to London's commitment to environmental stewardship.

However, the Centre faces challenges. Climate change, urbanization, and pollution pose ongoing threats to wetland habitats. The Centre also relies heavily on visitor income and donations to fund its conservation work.

"The London Wetland Centre is facing the same challenges as wetlands around the world," says Senior. "But we are determined to continue our work to protect these vital ecosystems. We believe that wetlands are not only essential for wildlife but also for people."

The future of the London Wetland Centre is bright. The Centre is committed to expanding its conservation programs, developing new educational initiatives, and engaging with a wider audience. The Centre is also exploring new ways to generate revenue, such as through sustainable tourism and green infrastructure projects.

"The London Wetland Centre is a beacon of hope for the future," says Maunder. "It shows that it is possible to create thriving ecosystems in urban environments, and it inspires us all to take action to protect our planet's precious biodiversity."

CHAPTER 73: LONDON'S GIN RENAISSANCE: FROM HISTORY TO CRAFT DISTILLING

The clink of ice in a glass, the sharp scent of juniper berries, and the subtle complexity of botanical infusions—these are the hallmarks of London's thriving gin scene. Once synonymous with the debauchery of the 18th-century Gin Craze, the spirit has undergone a remarkable transformation in recent years, fuelled by a resurgence of craft distilleries and a renewed appreciation for artisanal spirits. This chapter delves into London's role in the global gin renaissance, tracing the spirit's historical journey from mother's ruin to modern-day elixir and exploring the city's influence on the craft distilling movement.

The history of gin in London is a tale of two cities. In the 18th century, gin was the drink of the masses, a cheap and potent spirit that fuelled social unrest and moral panic. The Gin Craze, as it was known, was a period of widespread alcoholism and social disorder, immortalized in William Hogarth's iconic engravings "Gin Lane" and "Beer Street."

However, gin also has a more refined history. In the 19th century, gin evolved into a more sophisticated spirit, with distillers experimenting with new botanicals and refining their techniques. London Dry Gin, with its distinctive juniper-forward flavour profile, became a global standard, and brands like Beefeater and Gordon's rose to prominence.

"Gin has a long and fascinating history in London," says Jared Brown, Master Distiller at Sipsmith, one of London's pioneering craft distilleries. "It's a spirit that has been both vilified and celebrated, but its enduring appeal is undeniable."

The late 20th century saw a decline in the popularity of gin, as vodka and other spirits took centre stage. However, the turn of the millennium marked a turning point, with a new generation of craft distillers rediscovering the potential of Gin. These distillers, inspired by the farm-to-table movement and the growing demand for artisanal products, began experimenting with new botanicals and production methods, creating a wave of innovative and flavourful gins.

London, with its rich history of distilling and its vibrant bar scene, was at the forefront of this gin renaissance. The city's craft distilleries, often housed in railway arches, warehouses, and other unconventional spaces, became a symbol of the city's creative energy and entrepreneurial spirit.

"London's gin scene is a hotbed of innovation," says Zoe Burgess, Director of The Distillery, a bar and distillery in Notting Hill. "There's a real sense of community and collaboration among the city's distillers, and they are constantly pushing the boundaries of what gin can be."

The numbers speak for themselves. London is now home to over 50 distilleries, producing a wide range of gins, from classic London Dry to contemporary styles infused with exotic botanicals. Gin bars have also proliferated, offering a curated selection of gins from around the world and creative cocktails that showcase the spirit's versatility.

London's gin renaissance has had a significant impact on the global spirits industry. The city's distilleries have inspired a new wave of craft gin production around the world, from the United States to Japan. London's bartenders have also played a crucial role in popularizing gin cocktails, creating new and innovative drinks that have captured the imagination of drinkers worldwide.

"London is a global leader in gin innovation," says Brown. "The city's distilleries and bartenders are setting trends that are being followed around the world."

The gin renaissance is not just about flavour and innovation; it's also about sustainability and social responsibility. Many London distilleries are committed to using locally sourced ingredients, minimizing waste, and reducing their environmental impact. Some distilleries are also involved in community projects, supporting local charities and social enterprises.

"The gin industry is becoming more sustainable and socially responsible," says Burgess. "We are all aware of the impact our industry has on the environment and society, and we are committed to making a positive difference."

The London gin renaissance is a story of revival, innovation, and the enduring appeal of a classic spirit. It's a story that is still unfolding, with new distilleries, bars, and cocktails emerging all the time. As London continues to evolve as a global city, its gin scene will remain a vibrant and influential force, shaping the future of spirits and contributing to the city's rich cultural tapestry.

CHAPTER 74: THE LONDON PLAN: STRATEGIC URBAN DEVELOPMENT FOR CLIMATE CHANGE

London, a city with a rich historical tapestry, is weaving a new narrative—one of resilience, sustainability, and innovation in the face of climate change. At the heart of this narrative lies the London Plan, a strategic framework guiding the city's urban development. It's not just a blueprint for buildings and infrastructure; it's a vision for a city that thrives amidst environmental challenges, a model for sustainable urbanism in the 21st century.

The London Plan is a living document, constantly evolving to address the city's growing needs and the escalating climate crisis. In its latest iteration, the plan places a strong emphasis on climate change mitigation and adaptation, aiming to create a net-zero carbon city by 2030. This ambitious goal requires a radical transformation of London's energy systems, transportation networks, and building practices.

"The London Plan is a bold and ambitious vision for a sustainable future," says Shirley Rodrigues, London's Deputy Mayor for Environment and Energy. "It recognizes that climate change is the defining issue of our time, and it sets out a clear path for how London can become a global leader in climate action."

The plan's strategies are comprehensive and multifaceted. It calls for a significant increase in renewable energy generation, with a target of meeting 100% of London's electricity needs from renewable sources by 2030. The plan also promotes energy efficiency in buildings, aiming to reduce energy consumption and carbon emissions from the built environment.

"We need to decarbonize our energy systems and reduce our reliance on fossil fuels," says Rodrigues. "This is essential if we want to mitigate the worst impacts of climate change."

Transportation is another key area of focus for the London Plan. The plan aims to reduce car dependency and encourage the use of public transport, cycling, and walking. This is being achieved through a combination of measures, including the expansion of the public transport network, the creation of new cycle lanes and pedestrian zones, and the implementation of congestion charging schemes.

"We need to create a city where walking, cycling, and public transport are the preferred modes of travel," says Will Norman, London's Walking and Cycling Commissioner. "This will not only reduce emissions but also improve air quality and public health."

The London Plan also addresses the issue of urban greening. The plan calls for the creation of more green spaces, parks, and gardens, which can help to mitigate the urban heat island effect, absorb rainwater, and improve air quality. The plan also promotes the use of green roofs and walls, which can provide insulation, reduce energy consumption, and enhance biodiversity.

"Green spaces are essential for a healthy and sustainable city," says Rodrigues. "They provide a range of benefits, from improving air quality to promoting physical and mental well-being."

The London Plan is not without its challenges. The city's

rapid population growth and limited land availability make it difficult to implement some of the plan's ambitious targets. The plan also faces opposition from some developers and businesses, who argue that the strict environmental regulations stifle economic growth.

"The London Plan is a balancing act," says Professor Michael Batty, Chair of Urban Planning at University College London. "It's about finding the right balance between environmental protection, economic development, and social equity."

Despite these challenges, the London Plan is a beacon of hope in the face of climate change. It's a model for other cities around the world, demonstrating that it is possible to create a thriving and sustainable urban environment. The plan's success will depend on the continued commitment and collaboration of all stakeholders, from government agencies and businesses to community groups and individuals.

"The London Plan is a collective effort," says Rodrigues. "It's about all of us working together to create a better future for London."

The London Plan is a testament to the city's resilience, its ingenuity, and its commitment to creating a sustainable future. It's a roadmap for a city that is not only a global powerhouse but also a green, healthy, and equitable home for all its residents. The plan's vision is both ambitious and inspiring, a testament to the enduring spirit of London and its ability to rise to the challenges of the 21st century.

CHAPTER 75: LONDON'S TECH EDUCATION: CODING BOOTCAMPS AND DIGITAL SKILLS

The clatter of keyboards, the hum of collaborative brainstorming, and the glow of screens illuminating eager faces – these are the sounds and sights that characterize London's burgeoning tech education scene. As the world embraces the digital age, London has emerged as a leading force in shaping global tech education trends. The city's innovative approach to education, blending traditional academic institutions with cutting-edge coding boot camps and online learning platforms, is creating a new generation of tech talent and driving innovation across industries.

London's history of technological advancement is well-documented. From the Industrial Revolution to the development of the first computer, the city has always been at the forefront of innovation. However, the digital revolution of the 21st century has brought about a new set of challenges and opportunities, requiring a fundamental shift in the way we educate and train our workforce.

London has responded to this challenge with characteristic dynamism. The city has embraced a multifaceted approach to tech education, recognizing that there is no one-size-fits-all solution. Traditional universities, such as Imperial College London and UCL (University College London), offer world-class computer science and engineering programs, producing graduates who are sought after by top tech companies.

"London's universities are renowned for their academic rigor and research excellence," says Dr. Sue Black OBE, Professor of Computer Science at Durham University and a leading advocate for women in tech. "They are producing graduates who are well-equipped to tackle the challenges of the digital age."

However, London's tech education scene is not limited to traditional universities. The city has also seen a proliferation of coding boot camps, intensive training programs that equip students with the skills they need to enter the tech industry in a matter of months. These boot camps, such as General Assembly, Le Wagon, and Makers Academy, offer a more affordable and accessible alternative to traditional university degrees, catering to a wider range of learners.

"Coding boot camps are democratizing tech education," says Amali de Alwis, CEO of Code First Girls, a non-profit organization that provides free coding courses for women. "They are providing opportunities for people from all backgrounds to gain the skills they need to succeed in the tech industry."

London's tech education scene is also embracing online learning. Platforms such as Coursera, Udemy, and Codecademy offer a wide range of courses in coding, data science, cybersecurity, and other in-demand tech skills. Online learning offers flexibility and affordability, allowing people to learn at their own pace and from anywhere in the world.

"Online learning is revolutionizing the way we access education," says Anne Kiem, CEO of the Chartered Institute for IT. "It's making it possible for people to learn new skills and advance their careers without having to take time off work or relocate."

The impact of London's tech education initiatives is significant. The city's tech sector is thriving, attracting investment, talent, and businesses from around the world. London's tech companies are at the forefront of innovation, developing new technologies that are transforming industries and improving lives.

"London's tech education scene is a key driver of the city's economic growth and innovation," says Russ Shaw, founder of Tech London Advocates and Global Tech Advocates. "It's providing the skilled workforce that our tech companies need to thrive."

However, London's tech education scene still faces challenges. The demand for tech skills continues to outpace supply, and there are concerns about the lack of diversity in the tech sector. Women and ethnic minorities are underrepresented in tech, and there is a need for more targeted interventions to encourage their participation.

"We need to make tech education more inclusive and accessible to everyone," says de Alwis. "We need to break down the barriers that prevent women and minorities from entering the tech industry."

Despite these challenges, the future of London's tech education scene is bright. The city's commitment to innovation, its diverse talent pool, and its supportive ecosystem are all factors that will continue to drive the growth of the tech sector. As technology continues to evolve, London's tech education providers will need to adapt and innovate to meet the changing needs of learners and employers.

"The future of tech education is about lifelong learning," says Kiem. "We need to create a culture of continuous learning, where people can upskill and reskill throughout their careers. London is well-placed to lead this charge, with its world-class educational institutions, innovative start-ups, and diverse talent pool."

London's tech education scene is a testament to the city's ability to adapt and thrive in the digital age. It's a story of innovation, collaboration, and a commitment to providing everyone with the opportunity to succeed in the tech industry. As technology continues to transform our world, London's tech education sector will play an increasingly important role in shaping the future.

CHAPTER 76: LONDON'S SUSTAINABLE ARCHITECTURE: LEADING THE GREEN BUILDING REVOLUTION

In the heart of a city steeped in history, a new narrative of sustainability is being written. London's skyline, once dominated by Victorian grandeur and Gothic spires, is now punctuated by innovative structures that redefine what it means to be a modern, eco-conscious metropolis. This chapter delves into London's pioneering role in sustainable architecture, exploring how the city is integrating green building practices, renewable energy technologies, and innovative design strategies to create a more environmentally friendly and resilient urban landscape.

London's journey towards sustainable architecture is not a recent phenomenon. The city has long been a hub for architectural innovation, from the Crystal Palace of the 1850s, a marvel of iron and glass engineering, to the pioneering high-tech architecture of the Lloyd's building in the 1980s. However, the urgency of the climate crisis has accelerated London's embrace of sustainable design, pushing architects, developers, and policymakers to prioritize environmental considerations in urban development.

"London is at the forefront of the green building revolution," says Maria Smith, Director of Sustainability and Physics at Buro Happold, a global engineering consultancy. "The city is home to some of the most innovative and sustainable buildings in the world, and it is setting a new standard for sustainable urban design."

The evidence of London's green building revolution is visible across the city. The Bloomberg European Headquarters, completed in 2017, has been hailed as one of the most sustainable office buildings in the world. Its innovative design features include a "breathing" façade that regulates temperature, a rainwater harvesting system, and an integrated ceiling that combines heating, cooling, lighting, and acoustic functions.

"The Bloomberg building is a beacon of sustainable design," says Smith. "It demonstrates that it is possible to create a high-performance building that is also beautiful and functional."

Another example of London's sustainable architecture is the Siemens Crystal, a shimmering glass structure that houses the world's largest exhibition on urban sustainability. The Crystal features a range of sustainable technologies, including solar panels, ground source heat pumps, and rainwater harvesting systems. It is also designed to be energy-efficient, with a low carbon footprint.

London's commitment to sustainable architecture is not limited to iconic buildings. The city is also promoting green building practices in residential and commercial developments. The London Plan, the city's strategic planning document, sets out ambitious targets for reducing carbon emissions from buildings and encourages the use of sustainable materials and construction techniques.

"We need to make our buildings more energy-efficient and resilient to climate change," says Deputy Mayor for Environment and Energy, Shirley Rodrigues. "This is essential if we want to create a sustainable future for London."

London's green building revolution is not without its challenges. The high cost of sustainable technologies and materials can be a barrier for some developers. There is also a need for greater collaboration between architects, engineers, and policymakers to ensure that sustainable design is integrated into all aspects of urban planning.

"Sustainable architecture is not just about technology," says Smith. "It's about changing the way we think about buildings and cities. It's about creating spaces that are healthy, comfortable, and resilient to climate change."

Despite these challenges, London's commitment to sustainable architecture is unwavering. The city is investing in research and development, supporting innovative projects, and promoting education and awareness about sustainable design. London is also home to a growing community of architects, engineers, and urban planners who are passionate about creating a more sustainable future for the city.

"London is a city of innovation and creativity," says Rodrigues. "We are constantly pushing the boundaries of what is possible, and we are committed to creating a sustainable future for our city."

London's sustainable architecture is a testament to the city's forward-thinking approach to urban development. It's a model for other cities around the world, demonstrating that it is possible to create a thriving and sustainable urban environment. As London continues to evolve, its commitment to sustainable architecture will remain a key part of its identity, a symbol of its innovation, resilience, and dedication to a greener future.

CHAPTER 77: THE LONDON BOOK FAIR: SHAPING GLOBAL PUBLISHING TRENDS

The hushed murmur of negotiations, the rustle of turning pages, and the excited chatter of book lovers—this is the symphony of the London Book Fair (LBF), an annual spectacle that transforms the city into a global epicentre for the publishing industry. This literary extravaganza is not just a trade show; it is a catalyst for innovation, a platform for emerging voices, and a barometer of global publishing trends. In this chapter, we delve into the heart of LBF, exploring its role in shaping the international publishing landscape, its impact on the UK economy, and its ongoing evolution in the digital age.

LBF, founded in 1971, is one of the largest and most prestigious book fairs in the world. It attracts publishers, agents, authors, and booksellers from over 100 countries, creating a unique platform for networking, deal-making, and the exchange of ideas. The fair is a showcase for the latest books and literary trends, a forum for discussing the challenges and opportunities facing the publishing industry, and a celebration of the written word.

"The London Book Fair is the beating heart of the global publishing industry," says Jacks Thomas, Director of The

London Book Fair. "It's a place where the world of books comes together, where deals are made, where careers are launched, and where the future of publishing is shaped."

The LBF's influence on global publishing trends is undeniable. The fair serves as a barometer of the industry's health, reflecting the latest trends in genres, formats, and technologies. It's a place where publishers can showcase their latest titles, discover new talent, and negotiate international rights deals. The fair also hosts a series of seminars, workshops, and talks, providing a forum for industry professionals to discuss the challenges and opportunities facing the publishing world.

"The London Book Fair is a vital platform for the exchange of ideas and the promotion of international collaboration," says Thomas. "It's a place where the publishing industry can come together to discuss the future of books and reading."

The LBF's economic impact on London is significant. The fair generates over £200 million in economic activity for the city each year, through tourism, hospitality, and retail spending. The fair also supports thousands of jobs in the publishing, hospitality, and tourism sectors.

"The London Book Fair is a major contributor to the UK economy," says Stephen Lotinga, Chief Executive of the Publishers Association. "It's a showcase for British publishing, and it helps to attract investment and talent to the UK."

In recent years, the LBF has embraced the digital revolution, with a growing focus on digital publishing, audiobooks, and online content. The fair now features a dedicated Digital Zone, where exhibitors can showcase their digital products and services. The fair also hosts a series of events and seminars on digital publishing trends and technologies.

"The London Book Fair is evolving to reflect the changing landscape of the publishing industry," says Thomas. "We're embracing new technologies and formats, and we're creating new opportunities for publishers and authors to reach a global audience."

However, the LBF is not without its challenges. The rise of e-books and online retailers has disrupted the traditional publishing model, forcing publishers to adapt to a new era of digital consumption. The COVID-19 pandemic also had a significant impact on the fair, forcing it to go virtual in 2020 and 2021.

Despite these challenges, the LBF remains a vibrant and essential part of the global publishing industry. Its ability to adapt and innovate, combined with its rich history and global reach, ensures that it will continue to play a pivotal role in shaping the future of books and reading.

The London Book Fair is a testament to the enduring power of the written word and its ability to connect people across cultures and continents. It's a celebration of creativity, a catalyst for innovation, and a platform for the exchange of ideas. As London continues to evolve as a global cultural capital, the London Book Fair will remain a beacon of literary excellence, a testament to the city's rich publishing heritage, and a vital forum for shaping the future of the global book industry.

CHAPTER 78: LONDON'S VIETNAMESE COMMUNITY: FROM REFUGEES TO ENTREPRENEURS

In the vibrant tapestry of London's multicultural mosaic, the Vietnamese community shines as a testament to resilience, entrepreneurship, and cultural preservation. Their journey, beginning as refugees fleeing war-torn Vietnam and evolving into thriving business owners and integral members of British society, is a story of perseverance, adaptation, and the enduring human spirit. This chapter delves into the history, contributions, and evolving identity of London's Vietnamese diaspora, highlighting its impact on the city's social and economic landscape.

The narrative of London's Vietnamese community began in the late 1970s, as the aftermath of the Vietnam War triggered a wave of refugees seeking asylum. These early arrivals faced numerous challenges, including language barriers, cultural differences, and economic hardship. However, their determination to rebuild their lives and create a new home led to the establishment of a vibrant community that has since flourished.

"The Vietnamese community in London is a story of survival and triumph," says Thang Nguyen, Chairman of the An Viet Foundation, a leading Vietnamese community organization in the UK. "We arrived with nothing but the clothes on our backs, but we built a new life through hard work, perseverance, and a strong sense of community."

The heart of London's Vietnamese community beats in Hackney, where the streets are lined with Vietnamese restaurants, supermarkets, and shops. The aroma of pho, a traditional Vietnamese noodle soup, fills the air, while the sound of Vietnamese pop music spills out from local cafes. This bustling neighborhood, affectionately known as "Little Vietnam," is a testament to the community's entrepreneurial spirit and its desire to preserve its cultural heritage.

"Hackney is a vibrant hub for Vietnamese culture," says Thang Nguyen. "It's a place where we can connect with our roots, share our traditions with others, and contribute to the wider London community."

The Vietnamese community's impact on London's economy is undeniable. Vietnamese entrepreneurs have established a thriving network of businesses, ranging from restaurants and nail salons to grocery stores and import-export firms. These businesses not only provide essential services to the Vietnamese community but also contribute to the local economy, creating jobs and generating revenue.

"Vietnamese people are known for their hard work and entrepreneurial spirit," says Thang Nguyen. "We are proud to be contributing to London's economy and creating opportunities for our community."

Beyond economic contributions, the Vietnamese community has also enriched London's cultural landscape. Vietnamese cuisine, with its fresh ingredients, bold flavours, and healthy options, has become increasingly popular in recent years. Vietnamese restaurants, such as Pho and Viet Grill, have sprung up across the city, offering a taste of Vietnam to Londoners.

The Vietnamese community has also made its mark in the arts and entertainment scene. Vietnamese-British artists, such as filmmaker Hong Khaou and visual artist Tiffany Chung, have gained international recognition for their work, which often explores themes of identity, migration, and memory.

"The Vietnamese community is making a significant contribution to London's cultural diversity," says Dr. Thuy Tien Ho,a lecturer in Vietnamese studies at SOAS University of London. "We are bringing new perspectives, new stories, and new forms of artistic expression to the city."

However, the Vietnamese community in London also faces challenges. Discrimination and racism continue to be a problem for some, and the community is also grappling with issues of intergenerational conflict and cultural identity.

"We need to address the challenges facing our community," says Thang Nguyen. "We need to build bridges with other communities, promote cultural understanding, and ensure that our voices are heard."

Despite these challenges, the future of London's Vietnamese community is bright. The community is young, dynamic, and full of potential. With its strong work ethic, entrepreneurial spirit, and commitment to education, the Vietnamese community is poised to continue making significant contributions to London's social, cultural, and economic landscape. The community's success is a testament to the power of human resilience and the ability to adapt and thrive in a new environment.

CHAPTER 79: THE LONDON NIGHT-TIME ECONOMY: 24-HOUR CITY INITIATIVES

As the sun sets over London, a different kind of energy awakens. The city's streets come alive with the vibrant hum of nightlife, as pubs, bars, clubs, theatres, and restaurants cater to the desires of those seeking entertainment and social connection after dark. London's night-time economy is a complex and dynamic ecosystem, balancing the needs of businesses, residents, and visitors, while contributing significantly to the city's cultural identity and economic prosperity. This chapter delves into the complexities of London's 24-hour city initiatives, exploring the city's efforts to foster a vibrant and inclusive nightlife while mitigating the potential negative impacts on residents and communities.

London's night-time economy is a major economic engine, generating billions of pounds in revenue and supporting hundreds of thousands of jobs. The city's diverse range of nightlife options caters to a wide range of tastes and interests, from world-class theatres and music venues to cozy pubs and trendy bars. London's nightlife is also a melting pot of cultures, attracting people from all over the world to experience its unique atmosphere.

"London's nightlife is world-renowned," says Amy Lamé,

London's Night Czar. "It's a key part of the city's identity, attracting tourists and contributing to the city's vibrancy and diversity."

The city's 24-hour city initiatives aim to enhance and expand London's night-time offering, recognizing the potential for economic growth and cultural enrichment. The initiatives include measures to extend opening hours for businesses, improve transport links, and create safer and more welcoming environments for night-time revellers.

"We want to make London a truly 24-hour city," says Lamé. "A city that is safe, welcoming, and vibrant at all hours of the day and night."

The 24-hour city initiatives have already yielded positive results. The Night Tube, which provides 24-hour service on select Underground lines on weekends, has been a major success, making it easier for people to enjoy the city's nightlife. The Nighttime Commission, an independent body established to advise the Mayor of London on night-time matters, has also played a key role in shaping policy and advocating for the needs of the night-time economy.

However, the push for a 24-hour city is not without its challenges. The most significant of these is the potential impact on residents. Noise pollution, anti-social behavior, and increased traffic can all negatively affect the quality of life for those living near nightlife hotspots.

"The needs of residents must be taken into account," says Michael Kill, CEO of the Nighttime Industries Association (NTIA). "We need to find a way to balance the economic benefits of the night-time economy with the need to protect residents from its negative impacts."

The city is taking steps to address these concerns. The Agent of Change principle, a planning policy that places the onus on new developments to mitigate the impact of existing noise sources, is one example of how London is trying to strike a balance between the needs of businesses and residents.

"We are committed to working with businesses and residents

to create a nightlife that works for everyone," says Lamé. "We want to ensure that London's night-time economy is both vibrant and sustainable."

The future of London's night-time economy is uncertain, but the city's commitment to a 24-hour vision remains strong. The Nighttime Commission is working on a new 10-year strategy for the night-time economy, which will set out a vision for a more inclusive, diverse, and sustainable nightlife.

"We want to create a night-time economy that is for everyone," says Lamé. "A place where people from all walks of life can come together to enjoy the city's unique cultural offering."

London's night-time economy is a complex and multifaceted issue, with a wide range of stakeholders and competing interests. However, the city's commitment to finding a balance between the needs of businesses, residents, and visitors is a testament to its ability to adapt and innovate. As London continues to evolve as a global city, its night-time economy will undoubtedly play a crucial role in shaping its identity and its future.

CHAPTER 80: LONDON'S ROLE IN GLOBAL CLIMATE NEGOTIATIONS

The world watches as diplomats, scientists, and activists gather in London for the annual United Nations Climate Change Conference (COP). The stakes are high, the discussions intense, and the urgency palpable. As a global hub for finance, policy, and scientific research, London plays a pivotal role in shaping international climate policy, influencing negotiations, and driving action on climate change. This chapter delves into London's contributions to global climate efforts, examining its historical context, current initiatives, and its role in fostering international collaboration to address the climate crisis.

London's engagement with climate change is not a recent phenomenon. The city has a long history of environmental activism and policy innovation. The Great Smog of 1952, a catastrophic air pollution event, spurred the enactment of the Clean Air Act of 1956, a landmark piece of legislation that significantly improved air quality in the city. In recent decades, London has become a leader in climate action, implementing policies to reduce emissions, promote renewable energy, and adapt to the impacts of climate change.

"London is a global leader in climate action," says Shirley

Rodrigues, Deputy Mayor for Environment and Energy. "The city is committed to achieving net-zero carbon emissions by 2030 and is implementing a range of policies to make this happen."

London's role in global climate negotiations is multifaceted. The city hosts major international climate conferences, such as COP26, providing a platform for global leaders to discuss and negotiate climate action. London-based organizations, such as the Grantham Research Institute on Climate Change and the Environment, provide research and analysis that informs policymaking. The city's financial institutions are also playing an increasingly important role in financing climate-friendly projects and investments.

"London is a hub for climate finance," says Nick Robins, Professor in Practice for Sustainable Finance at the Grantham Research Institute. "The city's financial institutions are leading the way in developing innovative financial products and services that can help to accelerate the transition to a low-carbon economy."

London's influence on international climate policy is also evident in its own ambitious climate action plan. The city's policies, such as the Ultra-Low Emission Zone (ULEZ) and the congestion charge, have been effective in reducing emissions from transport, a major source of pollution in the city. London is also investing in renewable energy, with solar panels installed on public buildings and a growing number of wind farms being developed offshore.

"London is taking bold action on climate change," says Rodrigues. "We are implementing a range of policies to reduce emissions, promote renewable energy, and build a more resilient city."

However, London's efforts to tackle climate change are not without their challenges. The city's rapid population growth and economic development put a strain on resources and contribute to greenhouse gas emissions. The city also faces the challenge of adapting to the impacts of climate change, such as flooding and heatwaves.

"Climate change is a global challenge that requires a global response," says Robins. "London is playing its part, but we need to do more. We need to work together with other cities, governments, and businesses to accelerate the transition to a low-carbon economy."

The future of London's role in global climate negotiations is promising. The city is well-positioned to continue leading the way in climate action, with its expertise in finance, policy, and technology. London is also home to a vibrant community of climate activists and organizations, who are pushing for bolder and more ambitious action on climate change.

"London is a city that is not afraid to take on big challenges," says Rodrigues. "We are determined to create a more sustainable and resilient city, and we are committed to working with others to tackle the global climate crisis."

London's role in global climate negotiations is a testament to the city's commitment to a sustainable future. It's a story of innovation, collaboration, and the power of cities to drive change. As the world grapples with the urgent need to address climate change, London's leadership and expertise will be more important than ever. The city's actions will not only benefit its own residents but also serve as an inspiration and a model for other cities around the world.

CHAPTER 81: THE LONDON JAZZ SCENE: FROM RONNIE SCOTT'S TO NEW WAVE

The air is thick with the smoky allure of improvisation, the syncopated rhythms reverberate through dimly lit basements, and the soulful melodies transport listeners to another realm. This is the London jazz scene, a vibrant and ever-evolving tapestry of musical expression that has captivated audiences for generations. From the legendary Ronnie Scott's Jazz Club to the innovative sounds of the new wave, London's jazz scene has played a pivotal role in shaping global jazz culture, nurturing talent, and pushing the boundaries of musical creativity.

London's love affair with jazz began in the early 20th century, as American jazz musicians like Louis Armstrong and Duke Ellington toured the city, captivating audiences with their innovative sound and improvisational style. The 1930s and 40s saw the emergence of a homegrown British jazz scene, with musicians like George Chisholm and Kenny Baker blending American jazz influences with British traditions.

"London has always been a welcoming home for jazz," says Chris Philips, a jazz historian and author of *The History of*

Jazz in Britain. "The city's cosmopolitan atmosphere and open-mindedness have fostered a vibrant and diverse jazz scene."

The post-war era saw the opening of Ronnie Scott's Jazz Club in 1959, a Soho institution that would become synonymous with London's jazz scene. The club, co-founded by saxophonist Ronnie Scott and Pete King, hosted legendary performances by Miles Davis, Ella Fitzgerald, Nina Simone, and countless other jazz greats. It quickly became a mecca for jazz fans from around the world, and its legacy continues to this day.

"Ronnie Scott's is a national treasure," says Philips. "It's a place where jazz history was made, where generations of musicians honed their craft, and where audiences experienced the magic of live jazz."

The 1960s and 70s saw a flourishing of British jazz talent, with musicians like Tubby Hayes, Joe Harriott, and John Surman pushing the boundaries of the genre. The 1980s and 90s witnessed the emergence of a new wave of British jazz, influenced by funk, soul, and electronic music. Artists like Courtney Pine, Julian Joseph, and Jazz Jamaica brought a fresh and eclectic sound to the scene, attracting a new generation of jazz fans.

"The new wave of British jazz was a breath of fresh air," says Kevin Le Gendre, a music journalist and author of *Jazz Currents*. "It brought a new energy and vitality to the scene, and it helped to broaden the appeal of jazz to a wider audience."

Today, London's jazz scene is more diverse and vibrant than ever before. The city boasts a wide range of venues, from intimate jazz clubs to large concert halls, hosting performances by both established stars and emerging talent. The London Jazz Festival, an annual event that takes place across the city, is a major highlight of the global jazz calendar, showcasing the best of British and international jazz.

"London's jazz scene is incredibly diverse and dynamic," says Le Gendre. "There's something for everyone, from traditional jazz to cutting-edge experiments, from intimate club gigs to large-scale festivals."

London's jazz scene is not just about music; it's also about community and culture. Jazz clubs and bars have long been social hubs, places where people come together to listen to music, socialize, and connect with each other. The jazz scene also plays a vital role in supporting emerging talent, providing a platform for young musicians to showcase their skills and build their careers.

"Jazz is a communal music," says Philips. "It's about people coming together to create and share something special. London's jazz scene is a testament to that spirit of community and collaboration."

London's contribution to global jazz culture is undeniable. The city has nurtured some of the world's most talented jazz musicians, from Tubby Hayes and Joe Harriott to Courtney Pine and Shabaka Hutchings. London's jazz clubs and festivals have also played a crucial role in promoting jazz to a global audience, showcasing the diversity and richness of the genre.

"London is a global jazz capital," says Le Gendre. "It's a city that embraces jazz in all its forms, from traditional to avant-garde. It's a city that has nurtured some of the world's greatest jazz musicians, and it continues to be a hotbed for innovation and creativity."

CHAPTER 82: LONDON'S HALAL ECONOMY: MEETING THE NEEDS OF A DIVERSE POPULATION

The aroma of succulent grilled lamb skewers mingles with the fragrant scent of saffron-infused rice. Crowds gather at bustling stalls, eagerly sampling traditional delicacies like samosas, kebabs, and baklava. This is the vibrant world of London's halal economy, a dynamic sector that caters to the city's growing Muslim population and reflects London's commitment to inclusivity and diversity. This chapter delves into the growth and impact of halal businesses in London, examining their economic significance, cultural impact, and the challenges and opportunities they face in the modern era.

London's halal economy is a testament to the city's multiculturalism. With over 1.3 million Muslims, representing approximately 15% of the population, London is home to a large and diverse Muslim community. This community has created a demand for halal products and services, from food and fashion to travel and finance.

In response, a thriving halal economy has emerged, with businesses catering to the needs and preferences of Muslim consumers.

"The halal economy is a significant and growing part of London's economy," says Shelina Janmohamed, Vice President of Ogilvy Noor, a consultancy specializing in Muslim consumer insights. "It's a reflection of the city's diversity and its commitment to catering to the needs of all its communities."

The halal economy in London is estimated to be worth billions of pounds, generating employment and contributing to the city's economic growth. The sector encompasses a wide range of businesses, from small family-run restaurants and shops to large multinational corporations. Halal food is the most visible aspect of the halal economy, with hundreds of restaurants and takeaways serving up delicious and authentic halal cuisine from around the world.

"Halal food is more than just a dietary requirement," says Shelina Zahra Janmohamed, author of *Love in a Headscarf*. "It's a cultural expression, a way of connecting with our faith and heritage. London's halal food scene is incredibly diverse, offering a wide range of cuisines and flavours to suit every palate."

However, the halal economy goes far beyond food. It also encompasses fashion, cosmetics, pharmaceuticals, travel, and finance. Islamic fashion, with its modest styles and ethical principles, is gaining popularity among Muslim and non-Muslim consumers alike. Halal cosmetics, which are free from alcohol and animal-derived ingredients, are also in high demand.

"The halal economy is not just about food," says Janmohamed. "It's a lifestyle choice that encompasses all aspects of our lives. It's about ethical consumption, sustainable practices, and social responsibility."

The growth of the halal economy has had a significant impact on London's social and cultural landscape. It has created a sense of belonging and identity for the Muslim community, providing spaces and services that cater to their specific needs and preferences. The halal economy has also fostered greater cultural understanding and exchange between different communities, promoting diversity and inclusivity.

"The halal economy is a bridge between cultures," says Dr. H.A. Hellyer, a non-resident scholar at the Carnegie Endowment for International Peace. "It's a way for Muslims to engage with the wider community and showcase their culture and values."

However, the halal economy also faces challenges. One of the main challenges is the lack of standardization and regulation in the halal certification process. There are different certification bodies with varying standards, leading to confusion and mistrust among consumers.

"We need to establish a robust and transparent halal certification system," says Kirsty Henshaw, founder of Kirsty's, a halal-certified food brand. "This will not only benefit consumers but also help halal businesses to grow and thrive."

Another challenge facing the halal economy is the perception of Islamophobia and discrimination. Some businesses have reported facing barriers to entry and expansion due to negative stereotypes and prejudices.

"We need to challenge the negative stereotypes associated with Islam and the halal economy," says Janmohamed. "The halal economy is a positive force for good, creating jobs, promoting ethical consumption, and contributing to the diversity of our city."

Despite these challenges, the future of London's halal economy looks bright. The Muslim population in London is projected to continue growing, and with it, the demand for halal products and services. The halal economy is also becoming increasingly mainstream, with major retailers and brands recognizing the potential of this growing market.

"The halal economy is a global phenomenon," says Shelina Zahra Janmohamed. "It's not just about catering to the needs of Muslim consumers; it's about creating products and services that are ethical, sustainable, and inclusive. London is at the forefront of this movement, and its halal economy is poised to continue to grow and thrive in the years to come."

London's halal economy is a testament to the city's diversity, its entrepreneurial spirit, and its commitment to inclusivity. It's a vibrant and dynamic sector that is shaping the city's cultural and economic landscape. As London continues to evolve as a global city, its halal economy will remain a vital component of its identity, a symbol of its openness to different cultures and its commitment to building a more inclusive and equitable society.

CHAPTER 83: THE LONDON PODCAST INDUSTRY: SHAPING DIGITAL MEDIA

The soft glow of a microphone, the quiet buzz of editing software, and the intimate voices narrating stories, debates, and insights – this is the essence of London's thriving podcast industry. It's a new frontier in digital media, where creativity and technology converge, where voices from all walks of life can be heard, and where London has emerged as a global leader. This chapter delves into London's burgeoning podcast scene, exploring its rapid growth, its diverse content, and its impact on the evolving landscape of digital audio content.

London's rise as a podcasting powerhouse is a testament to its rich media heritage and its spirit of innovation. The city's long history of broadcasting, from the early days of radio to the present era of digital streaming, has fostered a deep-rooted culture of audio storytelling. This, coupled with the city's diverse population and entrepreneurial spirit, has created a fertile ground for the growth of the podcast industry.

"London is a natural hub for podcasting," says Matt Deegan, Co-Founder of the British Podcast Awards and Creative Director at Podot. "The city's rich media heritage, its diverse population, and its entrepreneurial spirit have all contributed to the growth of the podcast industry."

The numbers speak for themselves. London is now home to thousands of podcast producers, hosting a vast array of podcasts covering every imaginable topic, from current events and politics to comedy, history, and true crime. The city's podcasting scene is a reflection of its multiculturalism, with podcasts produced in multiple languages and catering to diverse audiences.

"London's podcast scene is incredibly diverse and vibrant," says Sam Shetabi, founder of the podcast network Acast. "There's a podcast for everyone in London, reflecting the city's rich cultural tapestry."

London's podcast industry is not just about entertainment; it's also a platform for education, information, and debate. Podcasts have become a powerful tool for independent creators, journalists, and activists to share their stories and perspectives with a global audience. They have also provided new opportunities for businesses and brands to engage with consumers in a more intimate and personal way.

"Podcasting is a democratizing force in media," says Ruth Fitzsimons, Managing Director of Podfront UK. "It's giving a voice to people who were previously excluded from traditional media outlets, and it's creating new opportunities for storytelling and audience engagement."

The economic impact of London's podcast industry is significant and growing. The UK podcast market is estimated to be worth over £1 billion by 2024, with London accounting for a significant share of this revenue. The industry supports thousands of jobs, from podcast producers and hosts to sound engineers and marketers.

However, the London podcast industry also faces challenges. The market is becoming increasingly crowded, with thousands of new podcasts launching each year. This makes it difficult for new podcasts to stand out and attract an audience. The industry is also grappling with issues of discoverability, monetization, and sustainability.

"The podcast industry is still in its early stages," says Deegan.

"There are many challenges ahead, but the potential for growth is enormous. We need to find new ways to support podcast creators, build sustainable business models, and ensure that the industry continues to thrive."

Despite these challenges, the future of London's podcast industry looks bright. The city's strong media infrastructure, its diverse talent pool, and its growing appetite for audio content are all factors that will continue to drive the growth of the industry. London is also home to a number of podcast festivals and conferences, such as The Podcast Show, which provide a platform for networking, learning, and collaboration.

"London is a global leader in podcasting," says Shetabi. "We are home to some of the most innovative and creative podcast producers in the world. I'm excited to see what the future holds for London's podcast industry."

London's podcast industry is a testament to the city's creativity, diversity, and entrepreneurial spirit. It's a powerful new medium for storytelling, information sharing, and community building. As London continues to evolve as a global media hub, its podcast industry will undoubtedly play an increasingly important role in shaping the future of digital audio content.

CHAPTER 84: LONDON'S QUANTUM COMPUTING HUB: THE NEXT TECH FRONTIER

In the quiet corners of London's academic institutions and tech labs, a revolution is brewing, one that promises to reshape our understanding of computation and revolutionize industries across the globe. Quantum computing, a field that harnesses the enigmatic principles of quantum mechanics to perform calculations beyond the capabilities of classical computers, is poised to be the next technological frontier. London, with its rich scientific heritage and thriving tech ecosystem, is at the epicentre of this quantum revolution, playing a leading role in research, development, and commercialization of this cutting-edge technology.

Quantum computing is not merely an incremental improvement on existing computing technologies; it's a paradigm shift. Unlike classical computers, which store information in bits that can be either 0 or 1, quantum computers use qubits, which can exist in multiple states simultaneously, thanks to a quantum phenomenon known as superposition. This allows quantum computers to perform complex calculations exponentially faster than classical computers, opening up new possibilities in fields like drug discovery, materials science, financial modeling, and artificial intelligence.

"Quantum computing has the potential to revolutionize every aspect of our lives," says Professor Peter Knight, a leading quantum physicist at Imperial College London. "It could lead to breakthroughs in medicine, energy, and materials science that were previously unimaginable."

London's quantum computing scene is a testament to the city's scientific prowess and its ability to attract and nurture top talent. The city is home to a number of world-leading research institutions, including the UCL Quantum Science and Technology Institute, the Imperial College Quantum Engineering Centre, and the National Quantum Computing Centre (NQCC). These institutions are conducting ground-breaking research in quantum algorithms, quantum hardware, and quantum applications, pushing the boundaries of what's possible with this revolutionary technology.

"London is a global hub for quantum research," says Professor Peter Leek, Director of the UCL Quantum Science and Technology Institute. "We have a critical mass of researchers working on all aspects of quantum computing, from fundamental science to practical applications."

London's quantum computing scene is not just about academic research; it's also about commercialization and real-world impact. The city is home to a growing number of quantum start-ups, such as Cambridge Quantum Computing (now part of Quantinuum) and Phasecraft, that are developing quantum software and algorithms for a variety of applications. These companies are attracting significant investment from venture capitalists and technology giants, demonstrating the commercial potential of quantum computing.

"London is a hotbed of quantum innovation," says Ilyas Khan, CEO of Quantinuum. "We are at the forefront of developing quantum technologies that will have a profound impact on industries around the world."

The UK government has recognized the strategic importance of quantum computing and is investing heavily in the sector. The National Quantum Technologies Programme (NQTP), a £1 billion initiative launched in 2014, aims to accelerate the development and commercialization of quantum technologies in the UK. The NQTP has funded a number of research centres, training programs, and industry partnerships, creating a vibrant ecosystem for quantum innovation.

"The UK government is committed to making the UK a global leader in quantum technologies," says Professor Knight. "We have the talent, the expertise, and the ambition to be at the forefront of this technological revolution."

However, London's quantum computing scene also faces challenges. The technology is still in its early stages of development, and there are many technical hurdles to overcome before quantum computers can be widely adopted. The shortage of skilled quantum scientists and engineers is also a concern.

Despite these challenges, London's quantum computing scene is poised for continued growth and innovation. The city's strong scientific foundation, its supportive ecosystem, and its entrepreneurial spirit are all factors that will drive the development of this transformative technology. As quantum computing continues to evolve, London is well-positioned to lead the way, shaping the future of tech and unlocking new possibilities for scientific discovery, technological advancement, and societal progress.

CHAPTER 85: THE CHANGING FACE OF CAMDEN: FROM PUNK ROCK TO TECH HUB

The rhythmic beat of the drums reverberates off the brick walls, the air is thick with the scent of leather and hairspray, and the crowd pulsates with the raw energy of youthful rebellion. This is the Camden Town of the 1970s and 80s, a haven for punks, goths, and other alternative subcultures, a vibrant scene that would leave an indelible mark on London's cultural landscape. Yet, Camden is not a static relic of the past; it is a dynamic and ever-evolving neighborhood, constantly reinventing itself to meet the demands of the modern era. This chapter delves into the fascinating metamorphosis of Camden, tracing its journey from punk rock mecca to emerging tech hub, and examining the complex interplay of forces that have shaped its identity.

Camden's countercultural roots run deep. The area's industrial past, with its canals and railway lines, provided a fertile ground for alternative communities to take root. In the post-war era, Camden became a magnet for artists, musicians, and bohemians, drawn by its affordable rents, eclectic atmosphere, and thriving music scene. The punk movement of the late

1970s found a spiritual home in Camden, with bands like The Clash, The Damned, and The Sex Pistols performing in iconic venues like the Roundhouse and the Electric Ballroom. Camden Market, with its eclectic mix of vintage clothing, handmade crafts, and alternative fashion, became synonymous with the neighbourhood's rebellious spirit.

"Camden was a place where you could be yourself," recalls Don Letts, filmmaker and DJ, who was a key figure in the punk scene. "It was a melting pot of creativity, a place where the underground could thrive."

As the decades passed, Camden's alternative scene continued to evolve, embracing a variety of subcultures, from goths and metalheads to ravers and hip-hop enthusiasts. The neighbourhood's music venues, such as the Jazz Cafe and Koko, hosted a diverse range of artists, while Camden Market continued to grow, attracting tourists and locals alike with its eclectic offerings.

However, the turn of the millennium brought about a significant shift in Camden's identity. The process of gentrification, driven by rising property prices and the influx of new residents and businesses, began to reshape the neighborhood. The opening of the Roundhouse as a state-of-the-art performance venue in 2006 marked a turning point, signalling a shift towards a more mainstream cultural offering.

"Gentrification is a double-edged sword," says Simon Pitkeathley, Chief Executive of Camden Town Unlimited, a business improvement district. "It has brought investment and revitalized the area, but it has also led to the displacement of some long-time residents and businesses."

The rise of the tech industry has also played a role in Camden's transformation. The area's proximity to King's Cross, a major transport hub and the home of Google's UK headquarters, has made it an attractive location for tech companies and start-ups. The Roundhouse now hosts regular tech events and conferences, and co-working spaces have sprung up throughout the neighborhood.

"Camden is becoming a magnet for tech talent," says Alex Stephany, CEO of Beam, a social enterprise based in Camden. "The area's creative energy, its diverse community, and its proximity to transport links make it an ideal location for tech companies."

The transformation of Camden is a complex issue, with both positive and negative consequences. On the one hand, the area has become more prosperous and diverse, with new businesses and cultural offerings. On the other hand, some long-time residents and businesses have been priced out, and there are concerns that Camden is losing its unique character and edge. The future of Camden is uncertain, but it is clear that the neighborhood is at a crossroads. It must find a way to balance the needs of its diverse community, preserve its cultural heritage, and embrace new opportunities for growth and development. The challenge for Camden is to maintain its spirit of creativity and rebellion while also adapting to the demands of the 21st century.

As London continues to evolve as a global city, Camden will remain a fascinating microcosm of its changing identity. The neighbourhood's story is a reminder that cities are not static entities, but rather dynamic and ever-changing landscapes shaped by the complex interplay of social, economic, and cultural forces. Whether Camden can successfully navigate these forces and retain its unique character remains to be seen, but its journey will undoubtedly provide valuable insights into the future of urban development and cultural preservation.

CHAPTER 85: THE CHANGING FACE OF CAMDEN: FROM PUNK ROCK TO TECH HUB

The rhythmic beat of the drums reverberates off the brick walls, the air is thick with the scent of leather and hairspray, and the crowd pulsates with the raw energy of youthful rebellion. This is the Camden Town of the 1970s and 80s, a haven for punks, goths, and other alternative subcultures, a vibrant scene that would leave an indelible mark on London's cultural landscape. Yet, Camden is not a static relic of the past; it is a dynamic and ever-evolving neighborhood, constantly reinventing itself to meet the demands of the modern era. This chapter delves into the fascinating metamorphosis of Camden, tracing its journey from punk rock mecca to emerging tech hub, and examining the complex interplay of forces that have shaped its identity.

Camden's countercultural roots run deep. The area's industrial past, with its canals and railway lines, provided a fertile ground for alternative communities to take root. In the post-war era, Camden became a magnet for artists, musicians, and bohemians, drawn by its affordable rents, eclectic atmosphere, and thriving music scene. The punk movement of the late

1970s found a spiritual home in Camden, with bands like The Clash, The Damned, and The Sex Pistols performing in iconic venues like the Roundhouse and the Electric Ballroom. Camden Market, with its eclectic mix of vintage clothing, handmade crafts, and alternative fashion, became synonymous with the neighbourhood's rebellious spirit.

"Camden was a place where you could be yourself," recalls Don Letts, filmmaker and DJ, who was a key figure in the punk scene. "It was a melting pot of creativity, a place where the underground could thrive."

As the decades passed, Camden's alternative scene continued to evolve, embracing a variety of subcultures, from goths and metalheads to ravers and hip-hop enthusiasts. The neighbourhood's music venues, such as the Jazz Cafe and Koko, hosted a diverse range of artists, while Camden Market continued to grow, attracting tourists and locals alike with its eclectic offerings.

However, the turn of the millennium brought about a significant shift in Camden's identity. The process of gentrification, driven by rising property prices and the influx of new residents and businesses, began to reshape the neighborhood. The opening of the Roundhouse as a state-of-the-art performance venue in 2006 marked a turning point, signalling a shift towards a more mainstream cultural offering.

"Gentrification is a double-edged sword," says Simon Pitkeathley, Chief Executive of Camden Town Unlimited, a business improvement district. "It has brought investment and revitalized the area, but it has also led to the displacement of some long-time residents and businesses."

The rise of the tech industry has also played a role in Camden's transformation. The area's proximity to King's Cross, a major transport hub and the home of Google's UK headquarters, has made it an attractive location for tech companies and start-ups. The Roundhouse now hosts regular tech events and conferences, and co-working spaces have sprung up throughout the neighborhood.

"Camden is becoming a magnet for tech talent," says Alex Stephany, CEO of Beam, a social enterprise based in Camden. "The area's creative energy, its diverse community, and its proximity to transport links make it an ideal location for tech companies."

The transformation of Camden is a complex issue, with both positive and negative consequences. On the one hand, the area has become more prosperous and diverse, with new businesses and cultural offerings. On the other hand, some long-time residents and businesses have been priced out, and there are concerns that Camden is losing its unique character and edge.

The future of Camden is uncertain, but it is clear that the neighborhood is at a crossroads. It must find a way to balance the needs of its diverse community, preserve its cultural heritage, and embrace new opportunities for growth and development. The challenge for Camden is to maintain its spirit of creativity and rebellion while also adapting to the demands of the 21st century.

As London continues to evolve as a global city, Camden will remain a fascinating microcosm of its changing identity. The neighbourhood's story is a reminder that cities are not static entities, but rather dynamic and ever-changing landscapes shaped by the complex interplay of social, economic, and cultural forces. Whether Camden can successfully navigate these forces and retain its unique character remains to be seen, but its journey will undoubtedly provide valuable insights into the future of urban development and cultural preservation.

CHAPTER 86: LONDON'S VEGAN VANGUARD: A PLANT-BASED REVOLUTION

In the bustling food scene of London, a culinary movement is taking root, one that is transforming the way we think about food and its impact on our planet. Veganism, a lifestyle that excludes all animal products, is thriving in London, with a burgeoning scene of restaurants, cafes, markets, and events catering to a growing population of plant-based eaters. This chapter explores London's role as a global leader in the vegan movement, examining its historical context, current trends, and its impact on the wider culinary landscape.

London's affinity for plant-based eating is not a new phenomenon. The city has a long history of vegetarianism, with the first Vegetarian Society founded in London in 1847. However, the vegan movement, which emerged in the mid-20th century, gained significant momentum in recent years, driven by growing concerns about animal welfare, environmental sustainability, and health.

"London is a global epicentre for veganism," says Toni Vernelli, International Head of Communications and Marketing at Veganuary, a global organization encouraging people to try veganism for January and beyond. "The city's diverse population, its innovative food scene, and its commitment to sustainability have all contributed to the rise of plant-based eating."

The numbers paint a compelling picture. London is home to hundreds of vegan restaurants, cafes, and shops, offering a wide range of plant-based cuisine, from traditional British fare to international dishes. The city's vegan scene is also vibrant and dynamic, with new establishments opening regularly and existing ones constantly innovating their menus.

"London's vegan food scene is world-class," says Merete Mueller, co-founder of the Vegan Life Live festival. "The city's chefs are incredibly creative and talented, and they are constantly pushing the boundaries of plant-based cuisine."

The rise of veganism in London is not just about food; it's also about lifestyle and ethics. Veganism is a philosophy that extends beyond diet, encompassing all aspects of life, from fashion and beauty to travel and entertainment. London's vegan community is diverse and active, organizing events, workshops, and campaigns to promote veganism and raise awareness of its benefits.

"Veganism is a movement for positive change," says Vernelli. "It's about creating a more compassionate, sustainable, and just world for all."

The impact of London's vegan scene on the wider food industry is significant. The growing demand for plant-based products has led to an explosion of vegan options in supermarkets, restaurants, and even fast-food chains. Major food companies, such as Unilever and Nestlé, have invested heavily in plant-based products, recognizing the growing market potential.

"The vegan movement is transforming the food industry," says Dominika Piasecka, spokeswoman for The Vegan Society. "It's forcing companies to rethink their products and practices, and it's creating new opportunities for innovation and growth."

However, the vegan movement in London also faces

challenges. The perception of veganism as niche or restrictive can be a barrier to wider adoption. The cost of vegan products can also be a deterrent for some consumers.

"We need to make veganism more accessible and appealing to everyone," says Mueller. "We need to show people that vegan food can be delicious, affordable, and convenient."

Despite these challenges, the future of veganism in London looks bright. The city's commitment to sustainability, its diverse population, and its thriving food scene are all factors that will continue to drive the growth of the vegan movement. As more and more people embrace a plant-based lifestyle, London is well-positioned to remain a global leader in veganism.

London's vegan scene is a testament to the city's openness to new ideas and its willingness to embrace change. It's a story of innovation, compassion, and the power of collective action to create a more sustainable and ethical food system. As London continues to evolve as a global city, its vegan movement will undoubtedly play an increasingly important role in shaping the future of food and influencing culinary trends around the world.

CHAPTER 87: THE LONDON UNMANNED AERIAL VEHICLE (UAV) INDUSTRY: NAVIGATING THE SKIES OF INNOVATION

In the boundless skies above London, a new era of aviation is quietly unfolding. Unmanned Aerial Vehicles (UAVs),commonly known as drones, are taking flight, transforming industries, capturing stunning aerial footage, and challenging traditional notions of transportation and surveillance. London, with its rich history of aviation innovation and its thriving tech ecosystem, is at the forefront of this drone revolution, shaping the global UAV industry and developing cutting-edge technologies that are poised to reshape our world.

The story of London's UAV industry is one of rapid advancement and regulatory evolution. In the early days of drone technology, the UK government was quick to recognize the potential of UAVs but also the need for robust regulations to ensure safety and security. The Civil Aviation Authority (CAA), the UK's aviation regulator, has played a crucial role in developing a regulatory framework for drones, striking a balance between innovation and public safety.

"London has a long history of aviation innovation," says David Black, Head of Innovation at the CAA. "We are committed to supporting the development of the UK's drone industry, while also ensuring that drones are operated safely and responsibly."

London's UAV industry is a diverse and dynamic landscape, encompassing a wide range of sectors, from aerial photography and videography to infrastructure inspection, delivery services, and even passenger transport. The city is home to a growing number of drone companies, such as Skyports, which is developing infrastructure for drone deliveries and air taxis, and Sensat, which uses drones to create digital twins of construction sites.

"London is a hub for drone innovation," says Duncan Walker, CEO of Skyports. "The city's unique blend of creativity, technical expertise, and supportive regulatory environment makes it an ideal place for drone companies to thrive."

The UK government has been proactive in supporting the development of the drone industry. The Future Flight Challenge, a £125 million government-funded program, aims to accelerate the development of autonomous aviation technologies, including drones. The government has also established a Drone Industry Action Group, which brings together industry stakeholders and policymakers to discuss the challenges and opportunities facing the sector.

"The UK government is committed to making the UK a global leader in the drone industry," says Black. "We are investing in research and development, supporting innovation, and creating a regulatory environment that is conducive to growth."

London's UAV industry is not just about technology; it's also about regulation and public acceptance. The CAA's regulatory framework for drones is one of the most comprehensive in the world, covering everything from pilot training and licensing to airspace restrictions and operational safety requirements. The CAA also works to educate the public about drone safety and responsible use.

"Public acceptance is crucial for the future of the drone industry," says Walker. "We need to ensure that drones are operated safely and responsibly, and that the public understands the benefits that drones can bring."

The potential applications of drones are vast and far-reaching. In the construction industry, drones are being used to survey sites, inspect infrastructure, and monitor progress. In agriculture, drones are being used to monitor crops, spray pesticides, and even plant seeds. In the delivery sector, companies like Amazon and DHL are experimenting with using drones to deliver packages.

However, the drone industry also faces challenges. One of the main challenges is the need for further technological development to improve the safety and reliability of drones. The lack of public awareness and understanding of drone technology is also a barrier to adoption.

"The drone industry is still in its early stages," says Black. "There are many challenges ahead, but the potential benefits are enormous. We need to continue to invest in research and development, educate the public, and work together to create a regulatory environment that supports innovation while ensuring safety."

London's drone industry is a testament to the city's innovative spirit and its ability to adapt to new technologies. It's a story of collaboration between industry, government, and academia, working together to unlock the potential of drones. As drone technology continues to evolve, London is well-positioned to remain a global leader, shaping the future of aviation and transforming the way we live and work.

CHAPTER 88: LONDON'S SOMALI COMMUNITY: CHALLENGES AND TRIUMPHS

The rhythmic beat of Somali music fills the air, mingling with the aroma of aromatic spices and the lively chatter of Somali language. Colourful traditional attire graces the streets as community members gather for Eid celebrations or cultural events. This vibrant scene is a snapshot of London's Somali community, a resilient and dynamic diaspora that has woven itself into the city's diverse tapestry. This chapter explores the challenges and triumphs of London's Somali population, delving into their history, cultural contributions, and ongoing efforts towards integration and empowerment.

London's Somali community is a relatively recent addition to the city's multicultural mosaic. The majority of Somalis arrived in the late 20th and early 21st centuries, fleeing civil war and instability in their homeland. They settled primarily in boroughs like Brent, Ealing, and Tower Hamlets, creating close-knit communities that provided support and a sense of belonging in a new land.

"The Somali community in London is a story of resilience and hope," says Dr. Kinsi Abdulleh, Director of the

Somali Development Services, a charity supporting Somali integration in the UK. "We have faced many challenges, but we have also achieved great things. Our community is a testament to the strength of the human spirit."

The Somali community has faced numerous challenges in its journey towards integration. Language barriers, cultural differences, and discrimination have posed significant obstacles. The community has also struggled with high unemployment rates, poverty, and social exclusion. However, despite these challenges, the Somali community has shown remarkable resilience and resourcefulness.

"We are a community that is proud of our heritage and culture," says Abdulleh. "We are also determined to overcome the challenges we face and build a better future for ourselves and our children."

The Somali community's contributions to London are significant and diverse. Somali entrepreneurs have established successful businesses in various sectors, from restaurants and shops to transportation and logistics. The community is also actively involved in civic and political life, with Somali-born individuals serving as councillors and community leaders.

"Somalis are making a positive contribution to London life," says Cllr. Hibaq Jama, a Labour councillor in Islington and a prominent Somali community leader. "We are doctors, teachers, business owners, and community activists. We are contributing to the city's economy and enriching its cultural diversity."

The Somali community has also brought a rich cultural heritage to London. Somali cuisine, with its aromatic spices and unique flavours, is gaining popularity across the city. Somali music and dance, with their vibrant rhythms and intricate movements, are showcased at cultural events and festivals. The Somali language, with its poetic beauty and rich oral tradition, is also being preserved and celebrated through community initiatives.

"Somali culture is a vibrant and dynamic part of London's

multicultural mosaic," says Abdulleh. "We are proud to share our traditions with the wider community and build bridges of understanding."

London's Somali community is a microcosm of the global Somali diaspora, which is estimated to number over 2 million people worldwide. London is one of the largest Somali diaspora communities in Europe, and its experiences and contributions offer valuable insights into the challenges and opportunities of diaspora communities.

The future of London's Somali community is one of continued growth and integration. The community is young and dynamic, with a strong entrepreneurial spirit and a commitment to education. As the second and third generations of British Somalis come of age, they are playing an increasingly important role in shaping the community's identity and its relationship with the wider society.

"The future of the Somali community in London is bright," says Jama. "We are a resilient and ambitious community, and we are determined to make our mark on this great city. We are here to stay, and we are here to contribute."

London's Somali community is a testament to the city's diversity and its ability to embrace different cultures. It's a story of resilience, adaptation, and the enduring power of the human spirit to overcome adversity. As London continues to evolve as a global city, its Somali community will remain a vital part of its identity, a source of creativity, innovation, and social progress.

CHAPTER 89: THE LONDON CIRCULAR ECONOMY: PIONEERING SUSTAINABLE BUSINESS MODELS

Amidst the sprawling urban landscape of London, a paradigm shift is underway. The city is not only embracing the circular economy but is also spearheading its development, transforming waste into resources and reimagining traditional business models. This chapter delves into London's pioneering role in the circular economy, exploring its innovative initiatives, the collaborative efforts of businesses and communities, and the city's commitment to a more sustainable and resilient future.

London's transition towards a circular economy is not merely a trend but a necessity. As the city's population grows and consumption patterns intensify, the pressure on resources and the environment is becoming increasingly evident. The circular economy, which aims to keep products, components, and materials at their highest utility and value at all times, presents a viable solution to these challenges.

"London is at the forefront of the circular economy movement," says Wayne Hubbard, CEO of the London Waste and Recycling Board (LWARB). "We are working with businesses, communities, and policymakers to create a more sustainable and resilient city by reducing waste, promoting resource efficiency, and fostering innovation."

London's commitment to the circular economy is enshrined in the London Plan, the city's strategic planning framework. The plan sets out ambitious targets for reducing waste, increasing recycling rates, and promoting the use of recycled materials in construction and manufacturing. The plan also encourages businesses to adopt circular business models, such as product-as-a-service and sharing platforms.

"The London Plan is a roadmap for a more sustainable and resilient city," says Shirley Rodrigues, Deputy Mayor for Environment and Energy. "It recognizes the circular economy as a key driver of economic growth and environmental sustainability."

London's circular economy is a diverse and dynamic ecosystem, encompassing a wide range of initiatives and stakeholders. The city is home to numerous businesses that are pioneering circular business models, such as the rental clothing platform Hurr Collective and the food-sharing app Too Good To Go. London is also home to a thriving network of community-based organizations, such as repair cafes and reuse hubs, that promote the sharing, repair, and reuse of goods.

"The circular economy is about creating a more equitable and sustainable society," says Sophie Thomas, founder of the circular design consultancy URGE. "It's about designing products and systems that are not just durable and repairable but also socially and environmentally responsible."

London's circular economy is not without its challenges. The transition to a circular economy requires a fundamental shift in our thinking and behavior. It also requires collaboration between businesses, government, and civil society. The lack of infrastructure and investment in circular economy initiatives can also be a barrier.

"The transition to a circular economy is not easy," says Hubbard. "It requires a concerted effort from all stakeholders. But the benefits are clear: a more sustainable environment, a more resilient economy, and a better quality of life for all."

Despite these challenges, London's circular economy is gaining momentum. The city's government is investing in circular economy initiatives, such as the Circular London program, which supports businesses to transition to circular models. London is also a member of the Ellen MacArthur Foundation's Network, a global platform for cities committed to accelerating the transition to a circular economy.

"London is leading the way in the circular economy," says Dame Ellen MacArthur, founder of the Ellen MacArthur Foundation. "The city's commitment to sustainability and innovation is an inspiration to us all."

London's circular economy is a story of hope and transformation. It's a story of a city that is reimagining its relationship with resources, waste, and the environment. It's a story of innovation, collaboration, and the power of collective action to create a more sustainable and equitable future.

As London continues to evolve as a global city, its circular economy will play an increasingly important role in its development. The city's commitment to sustainability and its pioneering work in the circular economy are setting a new standard for other cities around the world, demonstrating that a more sustainable and resilient future is within reach.

CHAPTER 90: LONDON'S INFLUENCE ON GLOBAL LGBTQ + RIGHTS

The rainbow flags flutter proudly in the breeze, a sea of vibrant colors surging through the streets of London. It's Pride month, a time of celebration, protest, and remembrance for the LGBTQ + community. In the heart of this jubilant crowd, one can feel the pulse of a city that has long been a champion for LGBTQ+ rights, a beacon of hope, and a catalyst for social change. This chapter delves into London's pivotal role in shaping global LGBTQ+ policies and culture, examining its historical context, legislative achievements, and ongoing activism.

London's history with LGBTQ+ rights is a complex narrative marked by both oppression and liberation. In the not-so-distant past, homosexuality was criminalized, and LGBTQ+ individuals faced discrimination and persecution. Yet, even in those dark times, London's underground LGBTQ+ community fostered spaces of resilience and camaraderie, laying the groundwork for future activism.

"The history of LGBTQ+ rights in London is a story of struggle and triumph," says Peter Tatchell, a veteran LGBTQ+ rights activist and founder of the Peter Tatchell Foundation. "From the clandestine bars of Soho to the landmark legal victories, we have fought tirelessly for our rights and our place in society."

London's journey towards LGBTQ+ equality has been marked by several landmark legal achievements. The decriminalization of homosexuality in England and Wales in 1967 was a watershed moment, albeit one that only applied to individuals over the age of 21. The 2004 Gender Recognition Act allowed transgender individuals to legally change their gender, while the 2010 Equality Act consolidated and strengthened existing anti-discrimination laws. In 2013, the UK became the 16th country in the world to legalize same-sex marriage, a hard-fought victory that was met with jubilation from the LGBTQ+ community.

"These legal victories were the result of decades of tireless activism and advocacy," says Tatchell. "They demonstrate the power of collective action to bring about social change."

London's influence on global LGBTQ+ rights extends far beyond its own borders. The city's activists and organizations have played a crucial role in shaping international LGBTQ + policy and advocacy. Organizations like Stonewall, founded in London in 1989, have campaigned for LGBTQ+ rights both domestically and internationally, providing support and resources to LGBTQ+ communities around the world.

"London has been a beacon of hope for LGBTQ+ people around the world," says Nancy Kelley, CEO of Stonewall. "Our city's vibrant and diverse LGBTQ+ community has inspired and supported movements for equality in countries where LGBTQ+ people still face discrimination and persecution."

London's cultural influence has also played a role in promoting LGBTQ+ acceptance and understanding. The city's vibrant arts scene, with its queer theatre, film, and music, has challenged stereotypes and provided a platform for LGBTQ+ voices. London's Pride parade, one of the largest in the world, is a celebration of LGBTQ+ identity and a powerful symbol of the community's resilience and visibility.

"London's cultural scene has played a crucial role in

normalizing LGBTQ+ identities and relationships," says Dr. Justin Bengry, a historian specializing in LGBTQ+ history. "It has helped to break down stereotypes and create a more inclusive and accepting society."

However, London's LGBTQ+ community still faces challenges. Discrimination, prejudice, and violence continue to be a reality for many LGBTQ+ individuals. The recent rise in hate crimes against LGBTQ+ people is a stark reminder that the fight for equality is far from over.

"We cannot be complacent," says Kelley. "We must continue to fight for our rights and the rights of LGBTQ+ people around the world. We must also work to create a society where everyone is free to be themselves, without fear of discrimination or violence."

The future of LGBTQ+ rights in London is one of continued progress and challenges. The city's diverse and vibrant LGBTQ + community is a source of strength and resilience, and its activism and advocacy continue to inspire others around the world. However, the fight for equality is ongoing, and London must continue to lead the way in promoting a more inclusive and accepting society for all.

CHAPTER 91: THE LONDON BLOCKCHAIN SCENE: CRYPTOCURRENCY AND BEYOND

The hum of computers working tirelessly, the digital buzz of online transactions, and the intellectual fervour of discussions around distributed ledger technology (DLT)—these are the sounds of London's blockchain scene. From the bustling offices of Level39 in Canary Wharf to the collaborative spaces of the London Blockchain Labs, London is at the forefront of the blockchain revolution, shaping the future of finance, technology, and even governance. This chapter dives into the multifaceted world of blockchain in London, exploring its origins, current advancements, and the city's pivotal role in the evolving landscape of this transformative technology.

London's embrace of blockchain is not a sudden phenomenon. The city's historical position as a global financial centre, coupled with its openness to innovation and supportive regulatory environment, has created a fertile ground for the development of blockchain technology and its applications.

"London is a natural home for blockchain," says Teana Baker-Taylor, Executive Director of Global Digital Finance (GDF), an industry body promoting the adoption of digital assets.

"The city's financial expertise, regulatory infrastructure, and openness to innovation have created a thriving ecosystem for blockchain companies and projects."

The London blockchain scene is diverse and dynamic, encompassing a wide range of activities, from cryptocurrency exchanges and trading platforms to decentralized finance (DeFi) protocols and blockchain-based supply chain solutions. The city is home to some of the world's leading blockchain companies, such as Elliptic, a blockchain analytics firm, and Copper, a digital asset custody provider. It's also a hub for blockchain start-ups and innovators, attracting talent and investment from around the world.

"London is a global leader in blockchain innovation," says Dr. Catherine Mulligan, Co-Director of the Imperial College Centre for Cryptocurrency Research and Engineering. "The city is home to a vibrant community of entrepreneurs, researchers, and investors who are pushing the boundaries of what is possible with blockchain technology."

The UK government has been proactive in supporting the development of the blockchain industry. The Financial Conduct Authority (FCA), the UK's financial regulator, has established a regulatory sandbox for fintech companies, including those working on blockchain-based solutions. The government has also launched initiatives such as the UK Digital Strategy and the National Blockchain Strategy, which aim to promote the adoption of blockchain technology and position the UK as a global leader in the field.

"The UK government is committed to fostering innovation in the blockchain sector," says Baker-Taylor. "We believe that blockchain has the potential to transform many industries and improve people's lives."

The impact of blockchain on London's economy and society is already evident. Blockchain technology is being used to streamline financial transactions, improve supply chain transparency, and create new digital assets. It has the potential to revolutionize industries like healthcare, real estate, and even voting systems.

"Blockchain is a game-changing technology," says Mulligan. "It has the potential to make our systems more efficient, transparent, and secure. It's also creating new opportunities for innovation and economic growth."

However, the blockchain revolution is not without its challenges. The technology is still relatively new, and there are concerns about its scalability, security, and environmental impact. The regulatory landscape is also evolving rapidly, creating uncertainty for businesses and investors.

"The blockchain industry is still in its early stages," says Baker-Taylor. "There are many challenges ahead, but the potential benefits are enormous. We need to work together to build a regulatory framework that supports innovation while ensuring consumer protection and financial stability."

Despite these challenges, the future of London's blockchain scene is bright. The city's strong financial infrastructure, its supportive regulatory environment, and its diverse talent pool are all factors that will continue to drive innovation in the blockchain sector. As blockchain technology matures and its applications become more widespread, London is well-positioned to remain a global leader in this exciting new field.

London's blockchain scene is a testament to the city's ability to embrace new technologies and drive innovation. It's a story of collaboration between industry, government, and academia, working together to unlock the potential of blockchain. As the world becomes increasingly digital, London's blockchain industry is poised to play a crucial role in shaping the future of finance, technology, and society as a whole.

CHAPTER 92: LONDON'S ROLE IN GLOBAL ANTI-TERRORISM EFFORTS

The chilling events of 7/7, the 2005 London bombings, left an indelible scar on the city's psyche. However, amidst the grief and shock, London emerged as a global leader in combating terrorism, demonstrating resilience, adaptability, and a commitment to safeguarding its citizens and values. This chapter delves into London's pivotal role in global anti-terrorism efforts, examining its strategic approach, innovative measures, and international collaborations in the face of evolving threats.

London's approach to counter-terrorism is multifaceted, encompassing a wide range of measures, from enhanced security and intelligence gathering to community engagement and prevention programs. The city's counter-terrorism strategy is based on the principle of "Prevent, Pursue, Protect, and Prepare," a holistic approach that addresses the root causes of extremism, disrupts terrorist plots, protects critical infrastructure, and prepares for potential attacks.

"London's counter-terrorism strategy is world-leading," says Sir Mark Rowley, Commissioner of the Metropolitan Police Service. "It's a comprehensive and integrated approach that draws on the expertise of a wide range of agencies and organizations."

One of the key pillars of London's counter-terrorism strategy is intelligence gathering and analysis. The Metropolitan Police's Counter Terrorism Command (SO15), one of the largest counter-terrorism units in the world, works closely with MI5, the UK's domestic security service, to gather intelligence on potential threats. This intelligence is then analysed and used to disrupt terrorist plots and prevent attacks.

"Intelligence is the lifeblood of counter-terrorism," says a senior MI5 officer who spoke on condition of anonymity. "It allows us to identify and disrupt threats before they materialize."

Another important aspect of London's counter-terrorism strategy is community engagement. The police and security services work closely with community leaders and organizations to build trust and encourage cooperation. This includes initiatives to counter extremist narratives, promote social cohesion, and provide support to vulnerable individuals who may be at risk of radicalization.

"Community engagement is essential for effective counter-terrorism," says Rowley. "We need to work with communities to build trust and understanding, and to ensure that everyone feels safe and secure."

London's counter-terrorism efforts are not confined to its borders. The city plays a leading role in international counter-terrorism cooperation, sharing intelligence and expertise with partners around the world. London is also home to a number of international organizations, such as the International Centre for the Study of Radicalisation and Political Violence (ICSR), that conduct research and analysis on terrorism and extremism.

"London is a global hub for counter-terrorism expertise," says Dr. Peter Neumann, Director of the ICSR. "The city's experience in dealing with terrorism has made it a valuable partner for other countries facing similar challenges."

However, London's counter-terrorism efforts are not without controversy. The use of surveillance technology, such as facial recognition and bulk data collection, has raised concerns about privacy and civil liberties. The Prevent strategy, which aims to prevent radicalization, has also been criticized for targeting Muslim communities and stigmatizing them.

"We need to ensure that our counter-terrorism measures are proportionate and do not infringe on fundamental rights," says Silkie Carlo, Director of Big Brother Watch, a privacy campaign group. "We also need to avoid alienating communities and ensure that our counter-terrorism efforts are based on trust and cooperation."

Despite these challenges, London's counter-terrorism strategy has been largely successful. The city has not experienced a major terrorist attack since 7/7, and the number of foiled plots has increased significantly. London's experience demonstrates that a comprehensive and integrated approach to counter-terrorism, combining intelligence, community engagement, and international cooperation, can be effective in mitigating the threat of terrorism.

The future of counter-terrorism is uncertain. The threat landscape is constantly evolving, with new technologies and tactics emerging all the time. However, London's experience shows that it is possible to stay one step ahead of the terrorists through vigilance, innovation, and collaboration. London's role in global anti-terrorism efforts is a testament to the city's resilience, its commitment to security, and its unwavering belief in the values of democracy, freedom, and tolerance.

CHAPTER 93: THE LONDON VINTAGE SCENE: FROM FASHION TO FURNITURE

London, a city steeped in history and tradition, has a unique affinity for all things vintage. From the bustling stalls of Brick Lane Market to the curated collections of high-end boutiques, London's vintage scene is a treasure trove of fashion, furniture, and collectibles from bygone eras. This chapter delves into the vibrant world of London's vintage scene, exploring its origins, its diverse offerings, and its influence on global vintage and retro trends.

London's love affair with vintage is not a recent phenomenon. The city's rich history and cultural heritage have fostered a deep appreciation for the craftsmanship and aesthetics of past eras. The Victorian era, with its ornate furniture and elaborate clothing, the Art Deco period, with its sleek lines and geometric patterns, and the mid-century modern movement, with its minimalist designs and functional forms, have all left their mark on London's vintage landscape.

"London is a vintage lover's paradise," says Wayne Hemingway MBE, co-founder of the vintage clothing brand Red or Dead and a leading figure in the UK vintage scene. "The city's diverse history and culture are reflected in its vintage offerings, from fashion and furniture to music and collectibles."

London's vintage scene is a diverse and dynamic ecosystem, encompassing a wide range of businesses, from independent shops and market stalls to online retailers and auction houses. The city's vintage shops offer a treasure trove of one-of-a-kind items, from Victorian gowns and Art Deco jewellery to mid-century modern furniture and retro vinyl records. London's vintage markets, such as Brick Lane Market, Portobello Road Market, and Greenwich Market, are a bustling hub of activity, where shoppers can browse through a seemingly endless array of vintage clothing, accessories, and homeware.

"London's vintage scene is a treasure hunt," says Amy Winston, owner of the vintage clothing shop Retromania. "It's about discovering unique pieces that tell a story, that have a history and a soul. It's about finding something that is truly special."

London's vintage scene is not just about shopping; it's also about community and creativity. Vintage fairs and events, such as the Frock Me! Vintage Fair and the Classic Car Boot Sale, bring together vintage enthusiasts from all over the city and beyond. These events offer a chance to browse through a wide range of vintage items, meet fellow vintage lovers, and celebrate the enduring appeal of vintage style.

"The vintage scene is a community," says Hemingway. "It's about sharing a passion for all things vintage, and celebrating the creativity and craftsmanship of the past."

London's influence on global vintage and retro trends is undeniable. The city's vintage shops, markets, and fairs are a source of inspiration for fashion designers, stylists, and trendsetters around the world. London's vintage scene has also been featured in numerous magazines, blogs, and social media platforms, further amplifying its global reach.

"London is a trendsetter in the vintage world," says Wayne Hemingway. "The city's vintage scene is constantly evolving, with new trends and styles emerging all the time. It's a place where the past and the present collide, creating a unique and vibrant fashion landscape."

The vintage scene is not just about nostalgia; it's also about sustainability and conscious consumerism. Vintage clothing and furniture are often made with higher quality materials and craftsmanship than their modern counterparts, making them more durable and long-lasting. Buying vintage also reduces the demand for new products, which can help to conserve resources and reduce waste.

"The vintage scene is a sustainable alternative to fast fashion," says Winston. "It's about buying quality items that will last, rather than disposable trends that will end up in landfill. It's about making conscious choices that are good for the planet."

The future of London's vintage scene is bright. The city's love affair with vintage shows no signs of abating, with new generations of shoppers discovering the joys of second-hand treasures. The rise of online platforms and social media has also made vintage more accessible than ever before, allowing people from all over the world to connect with London's vintage scene.

"The vintage scene is constantly evolving," says Hemingway. "It's a dynamic and exciting space, with new trends and ideas emerging all the time. I believe that the vintage scene will continue to thrive in London and around the world."

CHAPTER 94: LONDON'S APPROACH TO SMART CITY TECHNOLOGY: A BLUEPRINT FOR URBAN INNOVATION

In the heart of London, amidst the city's iconic landmarks and historic streets, a technological transformation is underway. London is embracing the concept of a "smart city," leveraging data and technology to improve the lives of its residents, enhance sustainability, and drive economic growth. This chapter delves into London's innovative approach to smart city technology, exploring its various initiatives, the challenges it faces, and its potential to shape the future of urban living.

London's journey towards becoming a smart city is rooted in a long history of innovation and adaptation. From the introduction of the world's first underground railway in 1863 to the implementation of the congestion charge in 2003,London has consistently embraced new technologies to address urban challenges. In recent years, the city has accelerated its efforts to become a smart city, leveraging data, connectivity, and digital technologies to create a more efficient, sustainable, and liveable urban environment.

"London is a global leader in smart city innovation," says Theo Blackwell, Chief Digital Officer for London. "We are using technology to tackle some of the city's biggest challenges, from traffic congestion and air pollution to energy efficiency and public safety."

One of the key pillars of London's smart city strategy is the use of data to inform decision-making and improve services. The city has invested heavily in data collection and analysis, using sensors, cameras, and other devices to gather information about everything from traffic patterns and air quality to energy consumption and crime rates. This data is then used to optimize traffic flow, improve public transport, identify pollution hotspots, and deploy emergency services more effectively.

"Data is the lifeblood of a smart city," says Blackwell. "It allows us to understand how the city works, identify problems, and develop solutions that improve the lives of Londoners."

Another key aspect of London's smart city strategy is the promotion of connectivity. The city is rolling out a high-speed broadband network that will provide fast and reliable internet access to all residents and businesses. This connectivity is essential for the development of smart city applications, such as smart energy grids, intelligent transport systems, and connected healthcare services.

"Connectivity is the foundation of a smart city," says Blackwell. "It enables us to create a digital infrastructure that can support a wide range of innovative applications and services."

London is also at the forefront of developing and deploying smart city technologies. The city is piloting projects such as smart streetlights that adjust their brightness based on traffic conditions, sensors that monitor air quality and noise levels, and smart bins that alert waste collection services when they are full. London is also exploring the use of artificial intelligence and machine learning to optimize traffic flow, predict energy demand, and improve public safety.

"London is a testbed for smart city technologies," says Blackwell. "We are constantly experimenting with new ideas and approaches, and we are sharing our learnings with other cities around the world."

London's smart city initiatives have already yielded tangible benefits. The city's air quality has improved significantly in recent years, thanks in part to the introduction of the Ultra-Low Emission Zone (ULEZ). The use of data and analytics has also helped to improve traffic flow and reduce congestion. London's smart city initiatives are not only improving the quality of life for residents but also attracting investment and talent to the city.

However, London's smart city journey is not without its challenges. One of the main challenges is ensuring that the benefits of smart city technology are shared equitably across all communities. There are concerns that the digital divide could exacerbate existing inequalities, with some communities being left behind in the digital revolution.

"We need to ensure that smart city technology benefits everyone," says Blackwell. "We need to bridge the digital divide and ensure that all Londoners have access to the opportunities that technology can offer."

Another challenge is the need to balance innovation with privacy and security. The collection and use of data raise important ethical and legal questions, and it is crucial that safeguards are put in place to protect individuals' privacy.

"We need to be transparent about how we collect and use data," says Blackwell. "We also need to ensure that our data is secure and that it is not misused."

Despite these challenges, London's commitment to becoming a smart city is unwavering. The city is investing in infrastructure, promoting innovation, and working with partners to create a more sustainable, equitable, and liveable urban environment. London's smart city initiatives are not just about technology; they are about people. They are about using technology to improve the lives of Londoners and create a better future for all.

CHAPTER 95: THE LONDON FREELANCE ECONOMY: SHAPING THE FUTURE OF WORK

In the bustling heart of London, a new work paradigm is taking shape. Beyond the traditional nine-to-five office jobs, a vibrant and dynamic freelance economy is emerging, reshaping the way Londoners work and live. This chapter delves into London's burgeoning freelance scene, exploring its origins, current trends, and its potential to redefine the future of work in the city and beyond.

The rise of the freelance economy in London is a reflection of broader global trends. The advent of digital technologies, the increasing demand for flexible work arrangements, and the growing desire for autonomy and work-life balance have all contributed to the rise of freelancing. London, with its diverse economy, entrepreneurial spirit, and thriving tech scene, has emerged as a natural hub for freelancers and independent professionals.

"London is a magnet for freelancers," says Julia Kermode, CEO of the Freelancer & Contractor Services Association (FCSA). "The city's diverse economy, its world-class infrastructure, and its supportive ecosystem make it an ideal place for freelancers to thrive."

The numbers paint a compelling picture. London is home to over 2 million freelancers, making up nearly 15% of the city's workforce. The freelance economy is a significant contributor to London's GDP, generating billions of pounds in revenue each year. The sector is also growing rapidly, with a 30% increase in the number of freelancers in London over the past decade.

"The freelance economy is a major driver of economic growth in London," says Kermode. "It's creating jobs, stimulating innovation, and contributing to the city's vibrancy and diversity."

The freelance economy in London is incredibly diverse, encompassing a wide range of professions, from creative industries like writing, design, and media to professional services like consulting, marketing, and technology. Freelancers in London are also diverse in terms of their backgrounds, experiences, and skill sets.

"The freelance economy is a reflection of London's diversity," says Emma Jones CBE, founder of Enterprise Nation, a support network for small businesses and self-employed people. "It's a place where people from all walks of life can come together and create their own opportunities."

London's freelance economy is not just about economic benefits. It also represents a fundamental shift in the way we think about work. Freelancing offers individuals greater flexibility, autonomy, and control over their work-life balance. It also provides businesses with access to a global pool of talent and the ability to scale their workforce quickly and efficiently.

"The freelance economy is transforming the way we work," says Kermode. "It's giving people more freedom and flexibility, and it's empowering them to take control of their careers."

However, the freelance economy is not without its challenges. Freelancers often face financial insecurity, lack of benefits, and social isolation. The COVID-19 pandemic has also had a significant impact on the freelance economy, with many freelancers experiencing a loss of income and job opportunities.

"The freelance economy is not without its risks," says Jones. "But it also offers enormous opportunities for those who are willing to embrace the challenges and take control of their own destiny."

The future of the freelance economy in London looks bright. The city's strong economic foundation, its supportive ecosystem, and its diverse talent pool are all factors that will continue to drive the growth of the sector. The rise of remote work and the increasing demand for flexible work arrangements are also likely to accelerate the growth of the freelance economy.

"The freelance economy is the future of work," says Kermode. "It's a more flexible, agile, and adaptable model that can meet the changing needs of businesses and workers. London is at the forefront of this trend, and it's paving the way for a new era of work."

London's freelance economy is a testament to the city's entrepreneurial spirit and its ability to adapt to changing economic and social conditions. It's a story of individuals taking control of their careers, businesses embracing new models of work, and a city reinventing itself for the digital age. As London continues to evolve, the freelance economy will play an increasingly important role in shaping the city's future, creating new opportunities for growth, innovation, and social progress.

CHAPTER 96: LONDON'S INFLUENCE ON GLOBAL URBAN AGRICULTURE

Amidst the sprawling urban landscape of London, a green revolution is taking root. A burgeoning movement of urban farms, community gardens, and rooftop allotments is transforming the city's relationship with food and nature. This chapter delves into London's pioneering role in urban agriculture, exploring how its innovative initiatives are inspiring cities worldwide to embrace sustainable food production and create greener, healthier, and more resilient urban environments.

London's embrace of urban agriculture is not merely a trend but a response to pressing challenges. Rapid urbanization, climate change, and concerns about food security have sparked a renewed interest in local food production and sustainable urban development. London, with its rich history of market gardens and allotments, is rediscovering its agricultural roots and leading the way in urban farming innovation.

"London is a global leader in urban agriculture," says Sarah Williams, founder of Incredible Edible Lambeth, a community-led food growing network. "The city's diverse range of urban farming initiatives, from rooftop gardens to community orchards, demonstrates the potential for urban spaces to become productive and sustainable food sources."

The scale and diversity of London's urban agriculture scene is impressive. Over 1,000 community gardens and allotments are scattered throughout the city, providing space for Londoners to grow their own food, connect with nature, and build community. Rooftop farms, such as Growing Underground in Clapham, utilize hydroponics and LED lighting to cultivate fresh produce year-round. Aquaponic farms, like the one at the Castle Climbing Centre in Hackney, combine fish farming with hydroponics to create a closed-loop system that produces both food and fertilizer.

"London's urban farms are not just about growing food; they are also about education, community building, and social enterprise," says Pam Warhurst CBE, co-founder of Incredible Edible Todmorden, a town in northern England that has become a model for community-led food growing. "They are showing us that it is possible to create a more sustainable and equitable food system, one that benefits both people and the planet."

The impact of London's urban agriculture initiatives extends far beyond the city's borders. The city's innovative approaches to urban farming have inspired cities around the world to embrace similar projects. For example, the Sky Greens vertical farm in Singapore, which uses a rotating system to maximize sunlight exposure, was inspired by a visit to London's Growing Underground.

"London is setting a global example for urban agriculture," says Idris Elba, actor and co-founder of the Farm Africa initiative, which supports small-scale farmers in Africa. "The city's commitment to innovation and sustainability is an inspiration to us all."

London's urban farming movement has not only inspired other cities but has also contributed to global knowledge and expertise in urban agriculture. The city's universities and research institutions are conducting cutting-edge research on urban farming, exploring topics such as soil health, crop yields, and the social and economic impacts of urban agriculture.

"London is a hub for urban agriculture research and innovation," says Dr. Andrea Verhoeven, a researcher at the Centre for Urban Agriculture and Biodiversity at Coventry University. "The city's universities and research institutions are generating valuable knowledge that can be applied to urban farming projects around the world."

However, London's urban farming movement is not without its challenges. Limited space, high land values, and the need for specialized knowledge and skills can be barriers to entry for aspiring urban farmers. The lack of a comprehensive regulatory framework for urban agriculture can also create uncertainty and hinder investment.

"We need to create a more supportive policy environment for urban agriculture," says Williams. "This includes providing access to land, financial support, and technical assistance to urban farmers."

Despite these challenges, the future of urban agriculture in London looks bright. The city's commitment to sustainability, its growing awareness of the importance of local food production, and its vibrant community of urban farmers are all positive signs. London is also home to a number of innovative start-ups and social enterprises that are developing new technologies and business models to support urban agriculture.

"The future of urban agriculture is in our cities," says Collins. "It's about reconnecting people with food, creating resilient communities, and building a more sustainable food system. London is leading the way, and it's showing us that a greener and more sustainable future is possible."

London's urban farming movement is a story of innovation, resilience, and the power of community. It's a testament to the city's ability to adapt and thrive in the face of challenges. As London continues to evolve as a global city, its urban farming movement will play an increasingly important role in shaping its future, ensuring that the city has a sustainable and secure food supply, while also creating a healthier and more connected community.

CHAPTER 97: THE LONDON ETHICAL FASHION MOVEMENT

In the bustling heart of London's fashion scene, a quiet revolution is underway. Beyond the glitz and glamour of the runways, a growing movement is challenging the industry's unsustainable practices and advocating for a more ethical and sustainable approach to fashion. This chapter explores London's pivotal role in the global ethical fashion movement, examining its origins, key players, and its impact on the industry's evolving landscape.

London's ethical fashion scene is a vibrant tapestry woven from threads of activism, innovation, and social responsibility. The city's rich history of textile production and fashion design, combined with its diverse population and global outlook, has created a fertile ground for the growth of ethical fashion.

"London is a global hub for ethical fashion," says Safia Minney MBE, founder of People Tree, a Fair Trade fashion pioneer. "The city's creative energy, its diverse community of designers, and its commitment to sustainability have all contributed to the rise of ethical fashion."

The London ethical fashion movement has its roots in the 1990s, when a growing number of designers and consumers began to question the environmental and social impact of the fashion industry. The Rana Plaza disaster in 2013, where over 1,100 garment workers died in a factory collapse in Bangladesh, further galvanized the movement, highlighting the urgent need for change.

"The Rana Plaza disaster was a wake-up call for the fashion industry," says Orsola de Castro, co-founder of Fashion Revolution, a global movement calling for greater transparency and sustainability in the fashion industry. "It forced us to confront the human and environmental cost of our clothes."

London has responded to this call to action with characteristic innovation and creativity. The city is home to a growing number of ethical fashion brands, such as People Tree, Stella McCartney, and Veja, that are committed to sustainable materials, fair labour practices, and transparent supply chains. These brands are proving that ethical fashion can be stylish, desirable, and commercially successful.

"Ethical fashion is not a niche market," says Tamsin Lejeune, CEO of Ethical Consumer, a research and campaigning organization. "It's a growing movement that is reshaping the fashion industry."

London's ethical fashion scene is not just about brands; it's also about education, advocacy, and consumer empowerment. Organizations like Fashion Revolution and the Ethical Fashion Forum are raising awareness about the social and environmental impacts of the fashion industry and campaigning for greater transparency and accountability. Consumer campaigns, such as Fashion Revolution Week, are encouraging people to ask #whomademyclothes and demand greater transparency from brands.

"We need to change the way we think about fashion," says de Castro. "We need to move away from a culture of disposability and embrace a more sustainable and ethical approach to fashion."

The impact of London's ethical fashion movement is far-reaching. It is influencing consumer behavior, with more and more people choosing to buy ethical and sustainable fashion. It is also putting pressure on brands to adopt more responsible practices. The London College of Fashion's Centre for Sustainable Fashion is a leading research centre, driving innovation and promoting sustainable practices in the fashion industry.

"The ethical fashion movement is changing the fashion industry for the better," says Dilys Williams, Director of the Centre for Sustainable Fashion. "It's forcing brands to rethink their practices and to consider the social and environmental impact of their products."

However, London's ethical fashion movement is not without its challenges. The fashion industry is complex and globalized, making it difficult to trace supply chains and ensure ethical practices. Greenwashing, the practice of making misleading claims about the environmental benefits of products, is also a concern.

"We need to be vigilant about greenwashing," says Lejeune. "We need to hold brands accountable for their claims and ensure that they are truly committed to sustainability."

Despite these challenges, the future of London's ethical fashion movement is bright. The city's commitment to sustainability, its creative energy, and its diverse community of designers and activists are all factors that will continue to drive the movement forward. As consumers become more conscious of the impact of their choices, the demand for ethical fashion is only set to grow.

"London is a global leader in ethical fashion," says Minney. "The city's commitment to sustainability and its vibrant fashion scene are a powerful combination. I believe that London will continue to be at the forefront of the ethical fashion movement for many years to come."

CHAPTER 98: LONDON'S APPROACH TO URBAN MENTAL HEALTH

The frenetic pace of city life, the relentless hustle and bustle, the constant bombardment of stimuli—living in a metropolis like London can take a toll on mental well-being. Yet, amidst the urban clamour, a growing awareness of mental health issues and a commitment to providing support are emerging. This chapter delves into London's approach to urban mental health, exploring the challenges faced by its diverse population, the innovative strategies being implemented, and the potential for the city to become a model for mental well-being in an urban environment.

London's mental health landscape is as diverse as its population. The city's inhabitants experience a wide range of mental health conditions, from common issues like anxiety and depression to more complex conditions like schizophrenia and bipolar disorder. Factors such as poverty, social isolation, discrimination, and trauma can all contribute to poor mental health.

"London's mental health challenges are multifaceted and complex," says Dr. Jacqui Dyer MBE, Mental Health Tsar for the

Mayor of London. "The city's diversity, its fast-paced lifestyle, and its economic inequalities can all take a toll on mental well-being."

In response to these challenges, London has adopted a multi-pronged approach to mental health, focusing on prevention, early intervention, and accessible treatment. The city's Thrive LDN initiative, launched in 2017, aims to improve the mental health and well-being of all Londoners by creating a citywide movement for change. Thrive LDN brings together a wide range of stakeholders, including local authorities, the NHS, businesses, community groups, and individuals, to address the root causes of mental health problems and promote positive mental well-being.

"Thrive LDN is a unique initiative," says Dyer. "It's about creating a city where everyone feels supported and empowered to look after their mental health. It's about tackling the stigma associated with mental illness and creating a culture of openness and understanding."

One of the key pillars of Thrive LDN is the promotion of mental health awareness and education. The initiative is working to increase understanding of mental health issues, reduce stigma, and encourage people to seek help early. Thrive LDN is also supporting the development of community-based mental health services, providing easier access to support and treatment for those who need it.

"Early intervention is crucial for improving mental health outcomes," says Dr. Geraldine Strathdee, National Clinical Director for Mental Health at NHS England. "The earlier we can identify and treat mental health problems, the better the chances of recovery."

London is also at the forefront of innovative approaches to mental health care. The city is home to a number of pioneering initiatives, such as the Good Thinking online platform, which provides free mental health resources and support, and the Kooth online counselling service for young people. The city is also exploring the use of digital technologies, such as virtual reality and artificial intelligence, to deliver mental health interventions.

"London is a hub for innovation in mental health care," says Dyer. "We are constantly looking for new and better ways to support people with mental health problems."

The impact of London's mental health initiatives is already being felt. The city has seen a significant increase in the number of people seeking help for mental health problems, and waiting times for treatment have been reduced. London is also making progress in reducing the stigma associated with mental illness, with more people feeling comfortable talking about their mental health and seeking help.

However, London's mental health challenges remain significant. The COVID-19 pandemic has had a devastating impact on mental health, with a sharp rise in anxiety, depression, and other mental health conditions. The economic fallout from the pandemic has also exacerbated existing inequalities, putting further pressure on the mental health of vulnerable groups.

"The pandemic has highlighted the importance of investing in mental health," says Dyer. "We need to build a more resilient mental health system that can cope with the challenges of the future."

Despite these challenges, London's commitment to tackling mental health remains strong. The city is investing in mental health services, promoting mental health awareness, and supporting innovative approaches to care. London is also working to create a more inclusive and supportive environment for people with mental health problems, tackling discrimination and stigma.

London's approach to urban mental health is a testament to the city's resilience, its compassion, and its commitment to creating a healthier and happier society. It's a story of innovation, collaboration, and the power of community to support those in need. As London continues to evolve as a global city, its approach to mental health will undoubtedly remain a key priority, ensuring that the city is not just a centre for economic and cultural activity but also a place where everyone can thrive mentally and emotionally.

CHAPTER 99: THE FUTURE OF LONDON: PROJECTIONS AND CHALLENGES

London, a city steeped in history, stands on the precipice of a new era, facing a future ripe with potential and fraught with challenges. This final chapter of "Londonology" peers into the crystal ball, exploring possible scenarios for London's development in the coming decades. While predictions are inherently uncertain, analysing current trends and potential trajectories can offer valuable insights into the forces shaping the city's destiny.

Demographics are a key factor in London's future. The city's population is projected to continue growing, reaching 10 million by the mid-2030s. This growth will be driven by natural increase and international migration, further diversifying London's population. This demographic shift presents both opportunities and challenges. On the one hand, a growing population can fuel economic growth and innovation. On the other hand, it puts pressure on housing, infrastructure, and resources.

"London's future is inextricably linked to its demographic trajectory," says Professor Les Mayhew, an expert in demographics at Cass Business School. "The city needs to plan for a growing and increasingly diverse population, ensuring that everyone has access to housing, jobs, and essential services."

The economy is another critical factor shaping London's future. The city is a global financial powerhouse, but it faces challenges from Brexit, technological disruption, and the rise of other financial centres. London will need to adapt to these changes, diversifying its economy and investing in new industries, such as technology, life sciences, and creative industries.

"London's economic future depends on its ability to innovate and adapt," says Rajesh Agrawal, Deputy Mayor of London for Business. "The city needs to embrace new technologies, attract talent from around the world, and foster a culture of entrepreneurship."

Climate change is perhaps the most pressing challenge facing London. The city is vulnerable to rising sea levels, extreme weather events, and heat waves. London needs to invest in resilient infrastructure, reduce its carbon emissions, and promote sustainable living. The city's ambitious goal of becoming a net-zero carbon city by 2030 is a testament to its commitment to climate action.

"London is taking the climate crisis seriously," says Shirley Rodrigues, Deputy Mayor for Environment and Energy. "We are implementing a range of policies to reduce emissions, improve energy efficiency, and build a more resilient city."

London's cultural landscape is also evolving. The city's diversity is one of its greatest assets, but it also presents challenges in terms of social cohesion and integration. London needs to continue to foster a culture of tolerance, inclusion, and diversity, celebrating its multicultural identity and ensuring that everyone feels welcome and valued.

"London's diversity is its strength," says Justine Simons OBE, Deputy Mayor for Culture and Creative Industries. "We need to celebrate our differences and work together to create a more inclusive and equitable society."

London's future is not predetermined. It will be shaped by the choices we make today. The city has the potential to become a model for sustainable, inclusive, and prosperous urban living. But it also faces significant challenges that will require bold action and innovative solutions.

Several scenarios are possible for London's future. In one scenario, London continues to thrive as a global city, attracting investment, talent, and businesses from around the world. The city embraces new technologies, such as artificial intelligence and automation, to drive economic growth and improve the quality of life for its residents. In another scenario, London struggles to adapt to the challenges of climate change and economic disruption. The city's infrastructure is strained, its economy stagnates, and social inequality increases.

"The future of London is in our hands," says Professor Tony Travers, Director of LSE London, a research centre at the London School of Economics and Political Science. "The choices we make today will determine the kind of city we want to live in tomorrow."

London's future is not just about economic growth or technological advancement. It's about creating a city that is liveable, sustainable, and equitable for all. It's about preserving the city's unique character and heritage while embracing the opportunities of the 21st century. It's about building a city that is a beacon of hope, a model for the world, and a place where everyone can thrive.

CHAPTER 100: LONDON'S GLOBAL LEGACY: REFLECTING ON THE CITY'S WORLD IMPACT

London. A name that reverberates through history, a city that has shaped the modern world in countless ways. As we conclude our exploration of Londonology, it is essential to reflect on the multifaceted influence that this great metropolis wields, not just on its inhabitants but on the global stage. London is a city of contrasts and contradictions, a melting pot of cultures, a powerhouse of innovation, and a crucible of challenges. It is a city that has faced adversity with resilience, embraced change with open arms, and consistently reinvented itself to remain relevant in an ever-evolving world.

Throughout this book, we have journeyed through London's diverse landscape, exploring its economic prowess, cultural vibrancy, political significance, and social complexities. We have delved into the city's history, traced its evolution, and examined the forces that have shaped its identity. We have also looked to the future, considering the challenges and opportunities that lie ahead for this global metropolis.

London's global legacy is a testament to its enduring spirit of innovation and adaptability. The city's financial sector, cantered in the Square Mile, is a driving force in the global economy, shaping markets and influencing financial trends worldwide. London's cultural scene, with its world-class museums, theatres, and music venues, is a beacon of creativity and artistic expression. Its political institutions, including the Houses of Parliament and Buckingham Palace, are symbols of democracy and tradition.

London's diversity is one of its greatest strengths. The city is a melting pot of cultures, languages, and religions, a place where people from all over the world come together to live, work, and create. This diversity is reflected in the city's food, music, fashion, and art, creating a vibrant and dynamic cultural landscape.

"London's diversity is its superpower," says Mayor Sadiq Khan. "It's what makes London the greatest city in the world."

However, London's success is not without its challenges. The city grapples with issues such as inequality, housing affordability, and social mobility. The Brexit vote in 2016 has also created uncertainty about London's future relationship with Europe and its place in the global economy.

"London faces significant challenges, but it also has enormous potential," says Tony Travers, Director of LSE London, a research centre at the London School of Economics and Political Science. "The city's future will depend on its ability to address these challenges and harness its strengths to create a more equitable and sustainable society."

London's global legacy is not just about its economic and cultural achievements. It's also about its role as a centre for education, research, and innovation. The city's world-class universities and research institutions are at the forefront of scientific discovery, technological advancement, and social progress. London is also a hub for social innovation, with a thriving ecosystem of social enterprises and community organizations working to tackle social challenges.

"London is a city that values knowledge and creativity," says Professor Alice Gast, President of Imperial College London.

"We are committed to using our expertise to make a positive impact on the world."

London's global legacy is also evident in its commitment to sustainability and environmental protection. The city has set ambitious targets to reduce its carbon emissions, improve air quality, and create a more resilient urban environment. London's green spaces, from the sprawling Royal Parks to the community gardens tucked away in quiet corners, are a testament to the city's commitment to preserving nature in the urban environment.

London's influence on the world is undeniable. The city has shaped global trends in finance, fashion, music, art, and technology. Its ideas, its culture, and its people have had a profound impact on the world.

"London is a global city with a global reach," says Travers. "Its influence extends far beyond its borders, shaping the world in countless ways."

As we look to the future, London's global legacy is poised to continue. The city's dynamism, its diversity, and its commitment to innovation and sustainability make it well-equipped to face the challenges and opportunities of the 21st century. London's story is far from over, and its impact on the world will continue to be felt for generations to come.